After Baptism

After Baptism

Shaping the Christian Life

John P. Burgess

Book design by Sharon Adams
Cover design by Pam Poll Graphic Design

First edition
Published by Westminster John Knox Press
Louisville, Kentucky

This book is printed on acid-free paper that meets the American National Standards Institute Z39.48 standard. ♾

PRINTED IN THE UNITED STATES OF AMERICA

05 06 07 08 09 10 11 12 13 14 — 10 9 8 7 6 5 4 3 2 1

Library of Congress Cataloging-in-Publication Data

Burgess, John P.
After baptism : shaping the Christian life / John P. Burgess.
p. cm.
ISBN 0-664-22884-4 (alk. paper)
1. Christian life—United States. 2. Christian life—Reformed authors. 3. Ten commandments—Criticism, interpretation, etc. 4. Christian ethics—Reformed authors. I. Title.

BV4501.3.B86 2005
268—dc22 2004057237

For my mother

Contents

Acknowledgments

Because every book is to some extent autobiographical, it reflects the particular (and limited) experiences of its author. But every book is also a collection of insights that one has gained from others along life's way, and so is also a testimony of gratitude. As I grow older, I am ever more aware of those persons who have graciously shaped my thinking.

Many of the ideas for this book grew out of a seminar on the history of the interpretation of the Ten Commandments that I cotaught with a New Testament colleague, Dale Allison. I am grateful for his scholarship and teaching and for his steady encouragement of mine. A presentation at the Society of Christian Ethics helped me clarify my thinking specifically about Reformed treatments of law and the Decalogue. Of particular value was the invitation to present portions of this material at Westminster Presbyterian Church in Lincoln, Nebraska, the congregation that I once served part-time, in which I was married, and in which my first child was baptized. My particular thanks goes to Carolyn Zeisset, who helped organize my stay, and to Roger and Sue Shoemaker, who (besides being my in-laws) were wonderful hosts. The warmth with which the congregation received my presentations and the thoughtful discussion that ensued persuaded me that my ideas were worth putting to paper.

I am thankful as well to the First Congregational Church of Litchfield, Connecticut, and its pastor, Edward Duffy, for the generous invitation to speak at the 2001 Litchfield Lectures, and to both Joseph Kennedy III at East Liberty Presbyterian Church and Lynn Cox at Eastminster Presbyterian Church in Pittsburgh, who graciously offered me opportunities to share this material with adult Christian education classes.

Stephanie Egnotovich, executive editor at Westminster John Knox Press, skillfully edited the book and guided it through the publication process; comments from the Press's anonymous reviewers led to several important revisions that improved the book. Pittsburgh Theological Seminary and its president, Carnegie Samuel Calian, have provided a creative and supportive context for my thinking. My secretary, Kathy Anderson, buoys my spirits and faithfully works on my behalf. I am especially thankful to my students; their willingness to let me try out my ideas on them constantly surprises and blesses me.

The counsel of my wife, Deborah Lynn Shoemaker Burgess, has assisted me immeasurably every step of the way. My debt to her extends well beyond her careful reading of the manuscript in its early stages, for she is always helping me think about, and claim, key disciplines and practices of faith for our life together. My daughters Hannah, Luisa, and Rachel have been a key part of this venture; in many ways, this book is written for them, in the hope that each of them will grow more fully into her baptismal identity.

One other woman has been on my mind as I have written: my mother, Elizabeth Anne ("Betsey") Bulger Burgess, who along with my father, now deceased, raised me in the Christian faith and taught me to love theology. Her loyalty and love over the years have sustained me more than she can imagine. I hope that this book will serve as one small token of my profound thanks to her.

Introduction

> Therefore, my beloved . . . work out your own salvation with fear and trembling; for it is God who is at work in you.
>
> Phil. 2:12–13

A group of parents meets at a church one evening. These parents are congregational leaders. They are actively involved in teaching Sunday school, leading a youth program, and organizing mission trips and camping trips in which their children can participate. But these parents are uneasy. They worry that North American culture will tempt their kids to abuse alcohol or drugs, to waste money on things that they don't need, or to think only in terms of self-interest and self-gratification. The parents ask themselves, Just what can the church do to help its children know the God who has claimed them in the waters of baptism and who spiritually sustains them in the Lord's Supper?

As they talk, they begin to think about the promises that they and the whole congregation made when their children were baptized. One father admits that he and his wife had their daughter baptized not because her baptism was important to them, but because they knew that it would please their own parents. A mother wonders aloud whether it would not have been better to put off the baptism of her now-teenage son until he was old enough to make the decision for himself: "He doesn't even come to church these days—I can't get him out of bed Sunday mornings. I don't think that his baptism means anything to him." These people wonder whether they or other members of the congregation really understood what they were promising when they presented children for baptism.

Churches—at least Orthodox, Catholic, and mainline Protestant churches—baptize babies, as Christians have done for centuries. These churches are not apt to change their practice anytime soon. But more and more fathers and mothers—and others in congregations too—are wondering just what baptism is all about. They vaguely understand that they want a way to bring their children to God and place them in his loving arms, but they also want to know: Is baptism the right way to present their children to God? And what should they be doing, what should their congregations be doing, now that their babies have been baptized and they and the members of the congregation have made these promises?[1]

It is a good sign when the church begins to worry again about the meaning of baptism. But the solution does not lie in discarding baptism or in restricting it just to sincere adult believers—because the problem is not with baptizing babies or with baptism in general but with what comes *afterward*. Traditionally, font has led to table; the church has prepared baptized children to come to the Lord's Supper, and it has believed that the Supper sustains and deepens baptismal identity. But the questions that parents raise about baptism also apply to the Eucharist. They worry that it too has become an empty gesture, a matter of merely going through the motions. As they see it, the church's challenge today is how to translate both baptism and Eucharist into a way of life whereby people might give glory to God and care for each other and the world.

It is clear to the parents at the church that evening that there is nothing mechanical about shaping children in this way of life. They know that they cannot expect the church to come up with a magic formula, such as better Christian education materials (as important as they are), or more effective ways of using video or new technologies. At the same time, they are unwilling to let the church off the hook. They will not let it shove off its responsibilities for Christian formation to a Holy Spirit that ought to be able to work miracles that the church cannot. These parents want to be assured that they—and the church as a whole—are not helpless, that there are things that they can faithfully do in order to help their children grow in the life of faith.

This book is about the church's responsibility to clarify for its members, beginning with its children, the shape of the Christian life. I challenge the church to look to the Spirit, who is active in baptism and the Eucharist, and to identify and claim key practices and disciplines of faith that the Spirit uses to deepen our baptismal identity. The church must continue to baptize its babies and to prepare them for the Eucharist. But it is also critically important that the church say anew what comes after baptism and accompanies the Eucharist—and, thus, say what it means to live the Christian life. In this book, I look specifically at challenges facing North American Christians, and I will argue that a fresh examination of the Ten Commandments in particular can help us identify specific practices and disciplines that we and our children need.

Sustaining Christian Identity Today

Baptism, the Eucharist, and the commandments offer basic orientation points for Christian existence. They suggest key practices and disciplines that give the Christian life solid shape for our time. Because of these practices and disciplines, the Christian life is never rudderless, and the Christian community is never in uncharted waters. Instead, the church has something definite and concrete to say to parents who gather in church parlors and basements and ask, "What should we do, so that we and our children can better live out our baptismal identity?"

The sacraments and the commandments remind us that being Christian is not only a question of what we believe but also and foremost a question of how we live. Christians are a people who *live out* their faith. Christians believe themselves to be called to a *way of life* that is guided by God's Holy Spirit. They wish to be conduits of the divine love that God has offered them and the whole world in the life, death, and resurrection of Jesus Christ.

Especially at the beginning of this new millennium, Christians in North America must give new and sustained attention to what constitutes a Christian way of life. This work has become more important than ever, because the church in North America increasingly finds itself in a post-Christian society.[2] Many of us are unable to say clearly what makes Christian identity distinctive; we need to think again about what makes the Christian life "Christian."

Sociologists and theologians have long debated the extent to which the church in North America has lost cultural privilege and establishment, and what that means for its future. On the one hand, theories of secularization that forty years ago predicted the inevitable decline of religion in modern, technological societies have largely been modified or abandoned; religion and new forms of spirituality continue to capture people's interest and involvement today. From this point of view, religion in North America is more vigorous than ever.

On the other hand, there is also little doubt that North American society has grown more pluralistic over the last forty years. Americans look at the world and see many religious options, and, like good consumers, they pick what works best for them. Christianity is no longer the only game in town, if ever it was. We are now living in a "spiritual marketplace."[3] Many people have advice, whether for sale or free, about how to live a spiritual life.

Just what does it mean to be Christian in a world in which Christianity is just one option out of many, and an option that itself comes in so many varieties? Why be Christian, and why be this kind of Christian? What is the way of life that Christians are called to cultivate, and how does that way of life distinguish them from the dominant values and loyalties of the larger society in which they find themselves?

Were we to seek assistance from traditional summaries or systems of Christian theology, we would find their discussions of the Christian life typically under the broader heading of "sanctification," that is, the church's teachings about how individuals grow and develop in Christian faith. Consideration of the Christian life has generally come subsequent to the church's teachings about Christ, while preceding the church's teachings about church and sacraments. In such theological systems, the work and person of Jesus is the key to defining the nature of the Christian life.[4]

But these traditional systems should not mislead us into thinking that the doctrines of Christ, the Christian life, and the church can be handled only in this order. Much theological thinking today insists that we should consider the Christian life as a part of our doctrine of the church—that to be a Christian is to be a member of a community that nurtures a distinctive identity in Jesus Christ. One never simply grows in faith as an individual, but rather in the context of a community with distinctive commitments. The Christian life requires us not only to know Christ, but also to discover what it means to be members of the *body* of Christ, the church.[5]

This renewed emphasis on the Christian life as life in community has given many Protestants impetus to recover the sacraments. We are learning again that the Christian life begins not with a set of abstract theological definitions but with the living Christ, who acts in congregations as they baptize children and adults in the name of the Father, and the Son, and the Holy Spirit, and as they gather around the Lord's Table. In the sacraments, the triune God makes covenant with us and invites us to make covenant with him and all his people. Today we are beginning to remember again that to be Christian is, as I earlier noted, not first of all to have mastered certain intellectual propositions, but to be marked as God's beloved child and to grow into ever deeper experiences and expressions of that love within a community of faith and its sacraments and practices.[6]

Thus, we might rephrase our questions about the Christian life in this way: What specifically does it mean to live out one's baptismal identity in a world that wishes to call us by other names than that of the triune God? This book argues that North American Christians, both individually and in their congregations, have reason to take baptism, the Eucharist, and the Ten Commandments more seriously than they sometimes have in recent generations. Christian parents and the church must work together to help a child recognize and confirm the identity that the risen Lord has given him or her. They must help a child to resist those powers and forces that would tell him or her to be something else. The very identity of the church is at stake in its efforts to sustain the Christian identity of its members, beginning with its children.

The Practices and Disciplines of the Commandments

As they work to sustain baptismal identity and a eucharistic life, North American Christians have rediscovered the notion of *practices and disciplines* of faith. We are coming to see again that the Christian life is neither a social given (as though being Christian were somehow equivalent to being a citizen) nor an impossible ideal (good for Jesus but not for us). While Christ has freely given us a new identity in him, we must grow more fully into that identity and allow it to claim us and to reshape every area of our life. We must be continually rehearsed and strengthened in our baptism, and must learn to participate in the Eucharist with ever greater integrity.[7] We live in the "already, not yet"—somewhere "between the times"—as we seek to become what we already are in Christ.

To grow in faith, we must submit ourselves to a training program. We need to practice and discipline ourselves in the self-giving love that characterizes Jesus Christ and our identity in him. Practices and disciplines of faith aim at shaping us at our core, our inner self—what theologians have traditionally called the soul. These exercises of faith move us away from sinful selfishness toward a sense of wonder and delight in the spiritual interconnection of all humanity, and of humans and the larger creation. They draw us away from a life driven by anger and malice toward a life guided by compassion and gentleness.

These practices and disciplines take personal effort. No one can live the faith for anyone else, and I hope that my explorations will be useful to individuals who seek to practice their faith more fully. But I am convinced that individual Christians also need the support and guidance of a larger community of faith. Each of us, for example, needs the sacraments to strengthen and sustain us, and they are never simply private acts but, rather, a corporate participation in the life of Christ; even as they ask us to reshape our lives personally, they call us into a community of faith. Similarly, practices and disciplines of faith not only make personal demands but also connect us to a community that is called to embody Christ's way of life. This book thus aims at also stimulating pastors, church educators, seminary professors, and other church leaders to identify ways of life together that help families, small groups, and individuals discover a more faithful living of the faith. We must work together to encourage each other and hold each other accountable for the new life that we have received in Jesus Christ.

In my own tradition, the Reformed tradition that looks back to the Reformer John Calvin and such confessional statements as the Heidelberg Catechism of the sixteenth century and the Westminster documents of the seventeenth, the Ten Commandments have provided a handy rubric for defining and summarizing these personal and corporate practices and disciplines of Christian love and community. The commandments do not constitute a checklist of discrete, quantifiable activities that we can simply choose to do or not to do. Rather, they offer a set of ethical trajectories for Christian living, giving concrete shape to the identity that is now ours in Jesus Christ—and making explicit the contours of Christian love.[8] Training in the commandments enables Christian love to become more than a passing emotion. Instead, it becomes a way of life. The commandments call us back home to who we are in the eyes of God.

Christians, like Jews, have regarded the Ten Commandments as divided into two tables that summarize the entire law—that is, the will of God. In the Reformed counting (Jewish and Christian traditions have varied slightly in how they have identified and numbered the commandments), the first table has consisted of the first four commandments: "no other gods before me," "no graven images," "do not take the name of the Lord your God in vain," and "keep the Sabbath holy." The second table has encompassed the other six: "honor father and mother," "do not kill," "do not commit adultery," "do not steal," "do not bear false witness," and "do not covet."

The larger Christian tradition—and the Reformed tradition in particular—has carefully explored the interrelationship of these Ten Commandments and two tables. The first table has generally been understood to define our duties to God; the second, our duties to our neighbor. Christian theology has also correlated these two tables with Jesus' great love commandment: The first table spells out what it means "to love the Lord your God with all your heart, soul, and mind"; the second table, "to love your neighbor as yourself" (see Matt. 22:34–40).

The division of the commandments into two tables does not mean that a solid, impermeable wall stands between them. Rather, the two tables interact dynamically; one table and its responsibilities inevitably spill over into the other. For example, the love that the first table asks us to give God is meaningless unless it leads to the love of neighbor with which the second table is concerned, and the worship of God, the central concern of the first table, cannot be right unless it sends us into greater service to the world, the concern of the second table. So in learning to love and worship God, we come to see and respect the image of God in the neighbor. Conversely, it is only as we learn to love the neighbor that we come to know the true character of God and therefore how best to worship and serve him. As the First Letter of John so eloquently states, "Those who say, 'I love God,' and hate their brothers or sisters, are liars; for those who do not love a brother or sister whom they have seen, cannot love God whom they have not seen" (1 John 4:20).

Are some of the commandments more important than others, and how do they fit together as a whole? Some Christian theologians have argued that the last nine commandments help to explicate the first; they tell us what it means to have the God of Israel and the church as the one and only true God.[9] Others have noted that obedience to the last commandment, "Do not covet," underlies obedience to the others. Not to covet is to render to God what is God's, and to the neighbor what is the neighbor's. Conversely, a life driven by coveting effectively undoes the Decalogue as a whole; we desire what is not truly ours, seeking to take from God what belongs to him alone (in so doing, we turn to other gods and fail to honor the true God, violating the first table) and seeking to take from others what properly belongs to them (so we kill, or commit adultery, or steal, etc., violating the second table).[10]

I believe that the fourth, fifth, and sixth commandments have particular significance for the Christian life, because they identify and summarize the major practices and disciplines that help Christians sustain their baptismal identity. If we think of the commandments as an archway, the first commandment lies at the bottom of one side of the arch, and the tenth commandment at the bottom of the other side. The other commandments rest on these two and lead the Christian disciple from the first to the tenth, and vice versa. The three in the middle—keeping Sabbath, honoring father and mother, and not killing—are the keystones that give the arch strength to bear the full weight of the Christian life.

What do I mean specifically? Keeping Sabbath summarizes the first table. When we make time for God by practicing worship—when we set aside our own agenda and open ourselves to God's—we learn what it means to have no other gods (the first commandment), to demolish idols (the second), and to speak rightly of God (the third). Similarly, not killing summarizes the second table. When we practice respect for life, when we work to break down walls of anonymity and hostility, we commit ourselves to the neighbor's good in every respect: right relationship (the seventh commandment), economic justice (the eighth), truth telling (the ninth), and right desire for the neighbor's well-being (the tenth).

The fifth commandment sits at the very top of the archway. It points to both tables, to both love of God and love of neighbor. Later I will argue that our first experiences of the faith are profoundly shaped in the family. In learning to honor father and mother, we learn to honor God (the first table). We learn about submitting to authority, insofar as it is truly authoritative for our lives. In learning to honor father and mother, we also learn what it means to honor the neighbor (the second table). The first neighbors that we encounter are our parents, and life in the family exercises tremendous influence on how we learn to treat others in general, both within and beyond the family.

Keeping Sabbath, honoring father and mother, and not killing suggest the value of all of the Ten Commandments for disciplining the Christian life. Like these three, the other commandments can be broadened and deepened, so that all ten reach into every area of the Christian life, ultimately touching both our internal dispositions and our external behaviors. The Decalogue suggests a lifetime of disciplined work for growing in the Christian faith, but it also provides a rule for measuring out our progress.

If the commandments stir us to live out our baptismal identity in and for the sake of the world, their corresponding practices and disciplines also lead Christians to the Eucharist. As the bread is broken and the cup is poured, Christians encounter in a particularly concentrated way the living Christ, to whom they now belong by virtue of their baptism. They receive again of the One who is himself self-giving love: "This is my body, given for you. This is my blood, shed for you." In the Eucharist, Christians are invited to enter more fully into the disciplined way of life that Christ makes possible in their baptism.

Eucharistic practice, like growth in baptismal identity, embodies nothing less than the way of the Ten Commandments. Because the Eucharist invites us to *rest* in God, it teaches us the deeper meaning of Sabbath keeping, the fourth commandment. Because the Eucharist calls us to patterns of mutual submission and interdependence, it opens to us the deeper meanings of the fifth commandment, teaching us to *honor* each other in the community of faith as spiritual "fathers" and "mothers" and brothers and sisters. Because the Eucharist teaches us to regard these brothers and sisters as part of one body, it also explicates the deeper significance of the sixth commandment—"Do not kill"—or, positively stated, that we must care for others and *respect* every life as a precious gift to be received, like Christ in the Eucharist, with utter thanksgiving.

The Way of Confession

In speaking to parents, the church must quickly add that pilgrimage in the Christian life will not be without trial and temptation. The truth is that we will regularly get off track; some days, we will take two steps back for every step forward. The church must help parents to understand that for them and their children to grow in baptismal identity is for them to discover a new hunger and thirst for the Eucharist, a new dependency on God's grace and forgiveness. Parents will discover not how to make their children more perfect, but how to pray for them and stand by them, and how to encourage them to pray and stand by others in others' times of spiritual trial.

One may question how well the church will do at this task; in our time, the North American church is perpetually tempted just to "satisfy people's needs." But the church must learn anew and teach anew that the Christian life is not just a matter of satisfaction and self-realization but also a matter of deep searching and longing—a searching and longing for the life that is truly ours in Christ yet that proves so elusive to us, especially under our conditions of wealth and prosperity and security as North Americans.

In such a world, we must rediscover that the most distinctive feature of our identity in Christ is nothing less than a growing capacity for confession, in both senses of the word. We will have to learn what it means to recognize and *confess our sins*: the shortcomings and limitations that keep us from claiming our baptismal identity as children of God and from living a eucharistic life. And we will have to learn again to *confess our faith*: to state worshipfully and with theological clarity what it means that a gracious God is at work in us, even and especially in our spiritual hunger and thirst as God's beloved children.

Baptism, yes—but then what? The church will truly be the church only when it lives by the orienting power of the Holy Spirit. The church dare not abandon its children to the whims of this age. It must baptize its babies, and having baptized them, must seek to shape them over a lifetime in the way of Jesus Christ. Baptism and the Eucharist, the commandments and their accompanying practices of faith, represent an incomparable legacy that the church should honor as it engages in this work. In the sacraments and the Decalogue, the church will find rich sources for renewing the Christian life and for resisting those aspects of North American culture that would define our true identity primarily in terms of material achievement and consumption.

May the church in a perilous time again be able to say in praise and adoration, "Thanks be to God for his indescribable gift!" (2 Cor. 9:15). Thanks be to God for the ability to say who we really are—and to live out who we really are—as men and women, boys and girls, baptized into the name of the triune God, Father, Son, and Holy Spirit.

Chapter One

Baptism

For unto us a child is born, unto us a son is given.
Isa. 9:6, KJV

The couple has waited for nine months. The past few nights have been especially hard. The mother can't make herself comfortable. Early one morning, she finally awakens to discover that her water has broken. Soon the couple is on the way to the hospital. While the mother's contractions slowly build over the next hours, the father feels mostly at loose ends. He coaches the mother's breathing; he stares out the hospital window as the mother dozes; he watches the monitors that track the baby's heartbeat. Time almost stops.

Then something suddenly happens, as though someone had hit a switch. The mother's labor is now in earnest. Nurses fly into the room, bustling about. They tell the mother not to push yet, just to wait a little longer. Somewhere in the midst of the activity, the father hears one nurse tell another that the doctor is on the way.

The couple knows that the critical moment is near. The father sees the sweat and exhaustion on his beloved's face. He feels so helpless. He encourages her; he barks out orders to her: "Breathe in . . . one, two, three . . . now, out! Again . . . one, two, three!" The doctor suddenly appears. She asks how the mother is doing and whether she can push. With whatever strength remains, the mother gasps and pushes, gasps and pushes. Pain washes over her, but the doctor speaks encouragingly. "I can see its head now. Just a little bit more! Come on, now, push!"

As a tiny head appears—then with one more push, shoulders—the moment of crisis passes. The father no longer holds his beloved. Instead, he stares in amazement at the wondrous creature, the living flesh, that the doctor is pulling out of the mother's body. Years later, many of these memories will seem hazy, but neither mother nor father will ever forget their first glimpse of that new life—a new being with its own boundaries, its own shape and mass and appearance.

The baby now lies in the doctor's hands. She hands the new father a pair of surgical scissors and asks him if he would like to snip the umbilical cord. Then she picks the baby up, and as that tiny creature gasps for air, the doctor declares, "It's a girl." The doctor is not quite ready to hand the baby over. She still has to check its vital signs and sponge it off. As the parents impatiently wait for their baby, the doctor pauses and asks them a question, "What's her name?" The mother, still lying on the delivery table, proudly declares, "Her name is Hannah. Hannah Ruth."

Or so it was when our first daughter was born. We spoke the name upon which we had decided many weeks before—and only then did the doctor, finally, place the baby on my wife's chest, where my wife could hold her close. Something similar happened when our next two daughters, Luisa Katherine and Rachel Elizabeth, were born. Each time, the doctor held the child, asked her name, and only then gave her over to us.

"Her name is . . ." A few months later the mother and the father are asked that question again. They stand in front of a congregation on a Sunday morning. Their baby is dressed in a white gown or one of her first fancy dresses, perhaps something pink and frilly. The parents too are all dressed up. They feel proud yet a bit awkward about being on display. The minister motions to them to gather by the baptismal font. He offers prayers, asking that the waters might "be a fountain of deliverance and rebirth."[1] Then he turns to the couple, just as the doctor once did, and asks, "What is this child's name?"

Those in the congregation are on the edge of their seats. They peer forward, hushed, craning their necks to look around and over the heads of those in the pews in front of them. Will the baby sleep peacefully, or will she begin to fuss? Will she lie quietly in the minister's arms, or will she squirm? How much water will the minister use? What will the baby do when the cold water touches her forehead? Together they hold their breath and wait.

"What is her name?" In ancient Christian tradition, the parents respond with the Christian name—that is, the given name—of the child. The baptism is no less valid or beautiful if they state the full name, "Hannah Ruth Burgess." But they could simply say, "Her name is

Hannah Ruth." In the hospital, the doctor had held the baby, then had given her to the mother. Now the parents hold the baby, then hand her to the minister. He scoops water into his hand and lets it run down the baby's face, three times perhaps, as he declares, "Hannah Ruth, I baptize you in the name of the Father, and the Son, and the Holy Spirit."

In the waters of baptism, the minister announces that that baby has a different last name. From that moment on, her name is no longer simply, "Hannah Ruth Burgess." From now on, we must also call her by her true name, "Hannah Ruth, child of the God who is Father, Son, and Holy Spirit." The birth certificate may say, "Hannah Ruth Burgess," but her Christian, given name has now been joined to the name of the triune God. She has been baptized into the death and resurrection of Jesus Christ. She has become a temple of the Holy Spirit. We must tell her to "call no one your father on earth, for you have one Father—the one in heaven" (Matt. 23:9).

Something truly remarkable has just happened here. We know that parents don't easily let go of their baby. Not just anyone can hold her. Grandparents and trusted friends, yes. Older siblings and certified child-care givers, perhaps. A nurse, a doctor—okay. Parents are particular because, after all, she is their baby, the fruit of the mother's womb. She is their baby, no one else's. And now, despite their determination to hold on to their child as long as they can, they have gently laid her in the hands of a man or woman dressed in strange robes, speaking strange words. Like Hannah in the Old Testament, they had long prayed and hoped and waited for this baby, but now they have brought her back before God. They have come to the temple to offer this child to the Lord.

It is easy to make baptism little more than a sentimental ritual of welcoming a newborn baby into a congregation. The pastor sprinkles a few drops of water on the baby's head and parades her up and down the aisle. Those in the pews smile approvingly, as the organist finds the register with tinkling bells and plays, "Jesus Loves Me." But baptism is not simply a gentle anointing that makes everything about that baby innocent and clean. Baptism is also a drowning and dying. We have every reason to be terrified by it, and every reason to want to protect our children from it. At our first birth, we came out of our mother's womb, hollering and screaming, and perhaps it is not inappropriate that a cute little baby dressed in a white linen dress should now holler and scream as she comes to new birth in God's kingdom. None of us takes on a new identity without some kicking and screaming.

Perhaps the parents sense the danger of this moment as they bring their child forward. They may even tremble and shake as they deliver their baby into the hands of the minister—because that baby is no longer just their baby, if ever it was. In the waters of baptism, that baby has received a new identity. "You are not your own. . . . You were bought with a price" (1 Cor. 6:19–20). "Put away your former way of life, your old self, . . . and be renewed in the spirit of your minds, and . . . clothe yourselves with the new self" (Eph. 4:22–24). "So you also must consider yourselves dead to sin and alive to God in Christ Jesus" (Rom. 6:11).

"What is her name?" "Her name is Hannah Ruth, child of the God who is Father, Son, and Holy Spirit."

Baptismal Identity

A baby, of course, cannot understand these things. Yet the power of infant baptism lies precisely in its dramatic proclamation that God has claimed us before we could say or do anything about it.

The baby grows into a child, the child into a woman. Someday she tries to imagine to herself what that moment was like so many years ago, when a father and mother, a baby, a minister, and a congregation gathered at a font on a Sunday morning. She tries to understand what she could not understand at the time: that God held her in his loving arms at the beginning of her life, while she was still weak and powerless. By God's grace, she may now know that she can trust in this God, who honored her with life and new life before she knew how to honor herself, let alone God or others. She may be confident that God will cradle her at the end of her life, when she is weak and powerless again.

Baptism is not a Christian Nobel Prize that recognizes our outstanding contributions to God or humankind. Rather, baptism declares that God has reached out to us, before we ever knew how to reach out to him or others. This God keeps reaching out to us despite our faults and failures. God wants relationship with us and will allow nothing to get in the way—"neither death, nor life, nor angels, nor rulers, nor things present, nor things to come, nor powers, nor height, nor depth, nor anything else in all creation" (Rom. 8:38–39).

God in his mysterious freedom has created us for himself and has called us to be his children: sons and daughters of the God who is in intimate, loving relationship within his very being, the triune God, Father, Son, and Holy Spirit. None of us is ever anything more than a little tiny baby in the eyes of God. We never grow up to become God's equal. We never become independent, self-sufficient creatures. Yet we need not despair at our seeming insignificance. God calls us "Son" or "Daughter" and invites us to call him "Abba." The triune God is a God who comes to those who are weak and helpless, and lifts them up. Moses reminded the people of Israel that it was

> not because you were more numerous than any other people that the LORD set his heart on you and chose you—for you were the fewest of all peoples. It was because the LORD loved you and kept the oath that he swore to your ancestors, that the LORD has brought you out with a mighty hand, and redeemed you from the house of slavery, from the hand of Pharaoh king of Egypt. (Deut. 7:7–9)

Paul would say something similar to Christians of his time: "God chose what is foolish in the world to shame the wise; God chose what is weak in the world to shame the strong; God chose what is low and despised in the world, things that are not, to reduce to nothing things that are, so that no one might boast in the presence of God" (1 Cor. 1:27–29).

Every time the church baptizes a baby, it testifies to a God who knows how to bring life out of death, strength out of weakness, and something out of nothing:

> Once you were not a people,
> but now you are God's people;
> once you had not received mercy,
> but now you have received mercy.
> 1 Pet. 2:10

Like Israel and the first followers of Christ, we too would be nothing, a people without name, home, or identity, had not God bestowed a new life and a new identity on us. We do not first have to create an identity and ask God to approve it, nor do we have to earn an identity and ask God to deliver it to us as our just wages. In Jesus Christ, God has already placed his seal of approval on us, before we could do anything about it. From the beginning, God has known us better than we will ever know ourselves: "It was you who formed my inward parts; you knit me together in my mother's womb" (Ps. 139:13). God has claimed us and identified us as his own.

Remembering Baptismal Identity

Martin Luther said that a Christian should begin each day by making the sign of the cross and saying, "In the name of God, the Father, the Son, and the Holy Spirit. Amen."[2] Luther knew that we are forgetful creatures. We are tempted every day to forget who we really are. Sin is not simply a matter of moral turpitude; it is our inevitable tendency to believe that we are something different from the self that God has called us to be. So we must begin each day by reminding ourselves that we have been marked by the cross and that we now bear a new name, the name of the triune God. As Luther declared, "Therefore let everybody regard his Baptism as the daily garment which he is to wear all the time."[3]

A secular, consumer culture tends to reduce temptation to a question of whether we will eat another piece of chocolate or spend another dollar on something that we don't really need. But the New Testament makes clear that temptation is not simply a matter of sensual or physical desire; temptation attacks our core identity. Inevitably, the temptations that we are able to recognize as temptations are trivialities, not crises of identity. The temptations that we are not able to see pose the greater dangers to us, and we usually miss them altogether.

When Jesus was baptized by John in the river Jordan, the Gospels tell us that the heavens were opened and a voice said, "This is my beloved Son, with whom I am well pleased" (Matt. 3:17). For a moment, Jesus' identity was crystal clear to him. But in the very next instant, the Spirit led him into the wilderness to be tempted by the devil. Jesus' core identity was put to the test. Twice the devil tried to redefine Jesus' identity: "If you are the Son of God, then . . ." At the end, Satan is more crass: "Fall down and worship me." Give yourself to me, and I will provide for you. Let me tell you who you really are, so that you never have to worry about it again.

To succumb to temptation is to succumb to identity crisis. We begin to wonder who we really are and what we are supposed to be doing with our lives. We begin to doubt that our lives are worth much. We see only our limitations and dwell on our failures. As our inner core weakens, we become vulnerable to powers and forces that are all too ready to tell us who we really are, promising us that we will never have to worry about it again. A lifestyle, a political allegiance, or a racial or class label comes to define us, instead of our baptism.

The mother and the father of that beautiful baby now sit at home. It is the end of the day. Evening has fallen. Dinner is cooking. The baby is sleeping, and calm fills the air. As the father and the mother gaze into their baby's tiny face, they take delight in the mystery of her very being. And then they suddenly begin to wonder what their baby will be like when she grows older. Memories of their own growing up flood over them, and a tinge of sadness colors their reverie. The father and the mother recall painful moments, moments when they struggled to know who they really were. They look at that precious baby, and part of them wants to do whatever it can to ensure that their child will never make the same mistakes that they did, that she will never know the same depths of desperation and depression that once plagued them as teenagers or young adults.

The problem is that their baby is not simply theirs. This baby will come to live her own life. She will make her own decisions and go her own ways. She will sometimes bring her parents delight and will sometimes cause them sorrow. They will find themselves holding their child in their prayers, because the day will come when there is no other way to hold her. The daily wonderment of the parents' life together with their "baby" will change into their daily bewilderment: "I wonder what she is doing today. I wonder if we will hear from her."

In her childhood and early adolescence, the daughter will argue with her parents more than once about something that she has said or done. The father and the mother, wondering what in the world their child was thinking, will say, "You know that you're not supposed to . . ." The child, now driven into a defensive posture, will likely protest, "But all my friends' parents let them . . ." The parents try to call their child back to her senses. They finally pull out their last arrow, the argument that should clinch their victory: "But you are a Burgess, and Burgesses don't do those sorts of things."

That argument will never be decisive, despite the parents' greatest hopes. No longer is that child just a Burgess. The parents cannot impose an identity on their child. They can only point her to the identity that God once gave her and still gives her. If the parents are wise, they will remember what happened many years earlier: "What is this child's name?" "Her name is Hannah Ruth, child of the God who is Father, Son, and Holy Spirit."

Practices That Sustain Baptismal Identity

How will the child remember who she really is? How will she come to claim this identity in the triune God for herself? How will she not lose herself in the many other identities that people want to impose on her, identities that can only lead her astray and violate her true self? "Lead us not into temptation," we pray. But even Jesus was led up by the Spirit into the wilderness.

The first temptation, the one that lies beneath all others, is the temptation to be what we are not. The serpent raised doubts in the minds of Adam and Eve about who they really were. Did not God want them to be like God? The great fall into sin was not first of all a horrendously perverse act that would make the front page of a newspaper today. Rather, it was a fall into a never-ending search for identity:

> Who am I? This or the other?
> Am I one person today, and tomorrow another?
> Am I both at once? A hypocrite before others,
> And before myself a contemptibly woebegone weakling?
> Or is something within me still like a beaten army,
> fleeing in disorder from victory already achieved?
>
> Who am I? They mock me, these lonely questions of mine.
> Whoever I am, thou knowest, O God, I am thine.[4]

German theologian Dietrich Bonhoeffer wrote these words from a prison cell in July 1944.[5] Bonhoeffer had been arrested in April 1943 for conspiratorial activities against the Nazi government. He would be executed on April 9, 1945, just days before the end of the war in Europe. As Bonhoeffer sat in prison and pondered the ravages of war and the loss of his freedom, he asked himself who he really was—and he remembered, as he had again and again over the months of imprisonment, that God alone knew.

During the Nazi years, Bonhoeffer was concerned about how to sustain not only his own but also others' identity in Christ. When Hitler was appointed chancellor on January 30, 1933, Bonhoeffer immediately warned of the dangers to the church. At stake was something more than political power. Christians in Germany would now have to resist a political order that wanted them to think of themselves in terms of race, nationality, and purity of blood—not their baptismal identity. In the days ahead, they would have to ask themselves again and again who they really were. They would have to practice remembering their identity in Christ.

Soon after Hitler came to power, Bonhoeffer moved to London, where he became pastor of two German-speaking congregations. He felt that he needed to get away from Germany for a while in order to make sense of what was happening there, and he also wanted to broaden his intellectual horizons. But as would happen again in 1939, when he visited America and was invited to remain, Bonhoeffer came to believe that God was calling him to be with the German people, even in the midst of their difficult circumstances. At the request of leaders of the Confessing Church, that part of the German Protestant Church that had aligned itself with the Theological Declaration of Barmen and against Hitler's efforts to control the church, Bonhoeffer returned to Germany in March 1935, agreeing to direct a seminary for young men in their final stages of ministerial preparation.

Although the Nazis had by then taken control of the universities, where the theological faculties were located, the German church had a second kind of training institute, the *Predigerseminar* ("preachers' seminary"). After five years of intensive academic preparation at the university, candidates for the ministry did field work for a year or two in a congregation or another pastoral setting.[6] They then entered one of these Predigerseminare, where they lived and studied together for six to twelve months prior to receiving a pastoral post. Unlike the theological faculties, the Predigerseminare were directly under control of the church. But the church itself was increasingly dominated by the German Christians, that group in the Protestant church friendly to Hitler and his policies. The Confessing Church therefore established five of its own Predigerseminare. Although they had no official status, they provided the one place in which the Confessing Church could work freely with its ministerial candidates and help shape their pastoral identity.

The seminary that Bonhoeffer directed was briefly located on the Baltic Sea, near the village of Zingst, but was soon moved to an old abandoned schoolhouse in the town of Finkenwalde, in an area of northeastern Germany that would be given to Poland at the end of World War II. Living conditions for Bonhoeffer and the first group of twenty-three seminarians were difficult. They had little privacy, there were few places to bathe, and some of the young men had to sleep in the hallways. Food was limited. One of Bonhoeffer's students later recalled the excitement of a March day in 1937 when the telephone rang and a voice announced, "This is the freight yard. A live pig has just arrived for Pastor Bonhoeffer."[7]

Bonhoeffer knew that the seminarians needed to be deeply rooted in their Christian identity if they were to survive the political pressures that would face them as ministers in Nazi Germany. Members of the Confessing Church were already being arrested. War loomed on the horizon. In the opening lines of his book *Life Together*, in which he later reflected on his experiences at Finkenwalde, Bonhoeffer noted that "the Christian cannot simply take for granted the privilege of living among other Christians."[8] Like Jesus, like other Christians, the seminarians would eventually have to leave each other to go live "in the midst of enemies," but memories of their time together would help sustain them.[9] The patterns of life that they had practiced together would bind them across the miles and years, for, as Bonhoeffer wrote, "What is denied them as a visible experience they grasp more ardently in faith."[10]

While in England, Bonhoeffer had visited several Anglican communities whose members practiced a common, monastic-like life. He had learned that Christian community should be organized around three sets of key practices and disciplines of faith. The first—and foundational—set of practices and disciplines was focused on the Scriptures. Two other sets of practices and disciplines followed: practices relating to how members of the community should treat each other and live together, and practices relating to the celebration of the Lord's Supper.

Practices and Disciplines of Attending to Scripture

Scripture was central to Bonhoeffer's community because it had become central to his life. Sometime in 1931 or 1932, just after his ordination and at the beginning of his new teaching and ministerial duties,

> something happened, something that has changed and transformed my life to the present day. For the first time I discovered the Bible. . . . I had often preached, I had seen a great deal of the church, spoken and preached about it—but I had not yet become a Christian. . . . It became clear to me that the life of a servant of Jesus Christ must belong to the church.[11]

Bonhoeffer believed that as members of the Predigerseminar immersed themselves in the Scriptures, they would learn to open themselves to God's living Word—a Word that would remind them of their true identity in Christ. He recognized as well that this devotion to the Word required rhythms of both time together and time apart: "Whoever cannot be alone should beware of community. . . . Whoever cannot stand being in community should beware of being alone."[12]

Each morning when the seminarians awoke, they remained silent until they gathered for morning devotions around the breakfast table. They were to hear God's Word in Scripture before they spoke their own words to each other. Morning devotions had four elements: The community prayed several psalms, the community heard extended readings of the Scriptures (at least a chapter of the Old Testament and half a chapter of the New), the community sang hymns, and then Bonhoeffer offered prayer on behalf of the community. Bonhoeffer was so concerned that the community hear the Scriptures speak for themselves that only on Saturdays did he offer a brief explication.

After a small breakfast, the seminarians meditated privately for half an hour on a selected Bible passage—the same passage for the entire week. Bonhoeffer encouraged them also to lift up personal prayers for themselves and the other members of the community. In the community devotions, the spoken word was central. In private meditation, each person came to the Word in silence.

Before the midday meal, Bonhoeffer and his students gathered for half an hour of singing. At the end of the day, just before retiring for the night, they gathered again, sometimes for as long as forty-five minutes, as in the morning. These evening devotions echoed the elements of morning prayer but also included common intercessions for the community and the world, petitions for mutual forgiveness, and prayers for preservation in the night.

Bonhoeffer emphasized that these daily practices deepened the community's appropriation of the Word. Over the course of a week, as in a Benedictine monastery, Bonhoeffer and the seminarians prayed all 150 psalms. Bonhoeffer believed that in praying the Psalms, the community was praying through Christ, for the Psalms represented the full range of emotions that Christ had experienced and that the church as his body now experienced. He argued that even the psalms of vengeance could be prayed if the community remembered that Christ himself had been tempted to take revenge on his enemies but had in the end suffered and died for them.

The readings from the two Testaments proceeded by the principle of *lectio continua*—that is, a book of the Bible was read consecutively from beginning to end. Bonhoeffer believed that the community would find its identity in the Scriptures only as it became familiar with its broad narrative, the history of God's people from the garden of Eden to the New Jerusalem.

> We are a part of that which once took place for our salvation. Forgetting and losing ourselves, we too pass through the Red Sea, through the desert, across the Jordan into the promised land. With Israel we fall into doubt and unbelief and through punishment and repentance experience again God's help and faithfulness. . . . I find salvation not in my life story, but only in the story of Jesus Christ. . . . Only in the Holy Scriptures do we get to know our own story.[13]

The community's identification with the broad narrative of Scripture was balanced by its openness to the specific Word that Bonhoeffer believed God spoke to each member of the community individually. Bonhoeffer asked the seminarians in their personal meditations to be alert to the single word or phrase of Scripture that took hold of them. He noted that "God's Word desires to enter in and stay with us. It desires to move us, to work in us, and to make such an impression on us that the whole day long we will not get away from it. Then it will do its work in us, often without our being aware of it."[14]

The singing of hymns, Bonhoeffer believed, also opened the community to God's living Word. While Bonhoeffer appreciated great music for its own sake, he insisted that the community's singing be fully in service of the hymns' words. The music should intensify their meaning, not become a distraction. Moreover, he wanted this singing to help the community discover its unity in Christ, as well as its unity with the wider church's song of praise and supplication that stretches across time and space. In order to emphasize this point, Bonhoeffer asked that the seminarians sing in unison rather than in parts.

Bonhoeffer offered similar reflections about prayer. The Scriptures should discipline and direct the way in which the community lifts up its joys and concerns to God. Bonhoeffer believed that God's Word inevitably evoked human response and became living and active in the community's words. As with Scripture reading, personal and corporate practices of prayer were to be held in balance. The individual's struggles and concerns should come to expression as much as the community's.

These practices and disciplines of the Word provided the basic structure of the day but did not exhaust it. Bonhoeffer was clear that the majority of the day was to be given over to work—in this case, the academic program (in which Bonhoeffer's lectures on pastoral care, preaching, and life in community were central).[15] Work itself could be understood as a form of devotion in which one forgot oneself and poured oneself into the world. Nevertheless, Bonhoeffer also recognized that work should have limits. In the evenings, he and the seminarians paused from their studies and enjoyed time to chat, make music, and even play games.[16]

Practices and Disciplines of Life Together

Practices and disciplines of the Word led to Bonhoeffer's second set of practices and disciplines—those relating to the ordering of life in community, or what has traditionally been called "church discipline."[17] Bonhoeffer believed that the Word shaped not only people's relationship with God but also their relationships with each other; life in the presence of God opened up time and space for people to be present to each other. Bonhoeffer treated these practices and disciplines of relationship under the rubric of "service."

According to Bonhoeffer, the principal service that members of the community owe each other is proclamation of the Word. Bonhoeffer is thinking here about mutual counsel and guidance, not the preaching that takes place from the pulpit. The word that we owe each other only becomes possible, however, as speaking is balanced by silence. Drawing on the example of medieval Benedictine monks, who spent much of the day in silence, Bonhoeffer recognized that undisciplined speech keeps us from hearing God's Word to us and from speaking God's Word to each other. Thus, practices and disciplines of speaking and of keeping silent are equally important.

Gossip and rivalry can quickly undo a community. One of the rules that Bonhoeffer instituted at Finkenwalde was that no one should speak about another person behind his back—and if you did, you were required later to go to that person and tell him what you had said about him. In his chapter on service in *Life Together*, Bonhoeffer reiterates that the first principle of life together is to hold one's tongue:

> Where this discipline of the tongue is practiced right from the start, individuals will make an amazing discovery. They will be able to stop constantly keeping an eye on others, judging them, condemning them, and putting them in their places and thus doing violence to

> them. . . . The view of such persons expands and, to their amazement, they recognize for the first time the richness of God's creative glory shining over their brothers and sisters.[18]

By holding my tongue, I guard against my tendency to justify myself. Life in community depends on a basic posture of humility, in which one does not insist on one's own rights but, rather, makes space for others, honoring their identity in Christ.

Bonhoeffer explored three additional disciplines that deepen this spirit of humility: listening to others, helping others, and bearing others' burdens. Like holding one's tongue, each makes space for the other in all his or her complexity both as a creature and as a sinner. Before we ever say a word to others, they must know that they are loved and respected, that their boundaries will not be violated, and that they will not be put to shame for who they are. According to Bonhoeffer, we are able to listen, help, and bear only because Christ himself listens, helps, and bears through us. As we listen, help, and bear, we grow in the image of Christ and set forth Christ to others. Others will be reminded of their identity in Christ not first by our words about the Word but by the Word that speaks through our posture of humility and openness.

When we listen, we give the other our fullest attention and put our own agenda aside. When we are ready to help, we allow others to interrupt our carefully planned schedules. When we bear with others, we maintain relationship with them, even where their personal peculiarities weigh on us—indeed, even where their actions violate us—"for the law of Christ is a law of forbearance. Forbearance means enduring and suffering. . . . One who refuses to bear that burden would deny the law of Christ."[19]

Silence prepares the way for speaking. Similarly, listening, helping, and bearing make authoritative exercise of community discipline possible. We must not only make space for others but must also be ready to redirect them to their true identity in Christ. Bonhoeffer believed that at critical junctures in a community's life, one person could recognize when another needed a word of comfort or a word of admonition. We must be willing to call each other back to life in Christ and his body, away from the selfish, self-destructive tendencies of sin. "This does not mean," Bonhoeffer wrote, "that the others are being disparaged or dishonored. Rather, we are paying them the only real honor a human being has, namely, that as sinners they share in God's grace and glory, that they are children of God."[20] There are times, then, when we must not spare our words. But we speak not in order to dominate others, but in order to remind them of the mercy of the One who has claimed them as his own.

Practices and Disciplines of Eucharist

In Bonhoeffer's vision of life together, practices and disciplines of mutual service lead naturally to a third set of practices and disciplines, which relate to the celebration of the Lord's Supper. The community at Finkenwalde celebrated the Eucharist once a month and saw it as a high point of its life together. In the Supper, Bonhoeffer wrote, the community claims its truest, deepest identity: "Here the community reaches its goal. Here joy in Christ and Christ's community is complete."[21]

Bonhoeffer's emphasis on the Supper flowed from his understanding of human sinfulness. As had medieval Benedictine monks, Bonhoeffer regarded pride as the root of all sin; it destroyed relationship with God and relationship between persons.[22] Correspondingly, practices and disciplines that sustained life together had to suppress pride and nurture humility. One must seek to be directed by God's Word, not by one's own desires; to serve others rather than to dominate them; to be reconciled to God and to others. This reconciliation then received its deepest expression in the Lord's Supper.

All the practices and disciplines at Finkenwalde were aimed at community reconciliation. But in the context of the Lord's Supper, Bonhoeffer lifted up an additional practice: confession. Bonhoeffer believed that no human act was more difficult than making confession. A person who confesses his sins is acknowledging that he is not what he would like to believe about himself—or what he would like others to believe about him. One's pride suddenly lies exposed. The practice of confession demands most of a person when he confesses his sins not in general, but concretely—and not simply to himself or even to God, but to another person. Nothing is more humbling, even humiliating, than letting another see our failings. And nothing is more liberating than hearing the Word of forgiveness that the brother or sister in Christ can offer us.

Bonhoeffer recognized that the practice of confession can easily be distorted. The temptation of insincerity faces those who make confession, and those who hear confession have to resist the temptation to use what they now know against the one who makes confession, to dominate him or her. But Bonhoeffer also insisted that the Lord's Supper could not be celebrated with integrity unless the community had prepared itself through self-examination. When Bonhoeffer recommended to the seminarians that they practice confession, many of them worried that he was being too "Catholic," and they resisted. Yet Bonhoeffer wanted confession to be regarded not as a new law but as a "breakthrough to new life."[23] A turning point in the community's life came when he asked one of the seminarians to hear his confession.[24] Before long, the whole community was following his example.

The practice of confession joins the two sacraments—baptism and the Lord's Supper. Like Luther, Bonhoeffer regarded confession of sin as "the renewal of the joy of baptism."[25] To the degree that confession breaks our pride, we become aware once again of our identity as people who die in Christ to an old life. To the degree that we live by the forgiveness of sins, we are raised with Christ to a new life. Confession makes it possible for us to remember our identity as sons and daughters of the God who is Father, Son, and Holy Spirit. Confession of sin also makes it possible for us to receive the Supper, which strengthens and confirms us in our baptismal identity.

Practices for the Church Today

Bonhoeffer's efforts at shaping life together remind us of the importance of practices and disciplines of faith that keep us rooted in our true identity. These practices and disciplines are not a "works righteousness" that creates that identity by our own efforts; rather, they are a means by which God confirms the identity that he bestowed upon us even from "before the foundation of the world" (Eph. 1:4).

Practices and disciplines of faith help us remain clear about who we really are. They mark us off as God's own, and they shape us. They help us grow more fully into the image of Christ. God's Spirit uses them to draw us more fully into the very life of God.[26] Led by God's Spirit, we participate in them in grateful response to God.

Christians in recent years have begun to rediscover the foundational value of such identity-confirming, identity-shaping practices and disciplines as prayer, Scripture reading, and the sacraments. Some follow the church's Puritan forebears in including Sabbath keeping and tithing. One recent book includes a number of other practices and disciplines that we might not normally think of: honoring the body, offering hospitality, dying well, and singing our lives.[27]

Bonhoeffer's three sets of practices and disciplines should not limit our imagination about what might count as a specific practice or discipline; rather, they can help us understand all of them as practices and disciplines of receiving God's *living Word* for today. In all three cases, the Word that we receive is more than human words; it is God's Word of promise, ultimately Jesus Christ, the risen Lord. Bonhoeffer's practices and disciplines invite us to know this Jesus, to be shaped more fully into his image, and to offer him to the world.

The first set of practices and disciplines opens us to the living Christ as he comes to us in Scripture and invites our response in prayer. So we pray the Psalms, read the two Testaments, sing our praises, and lift up our prayers of joy and concern. Bonhoeffer's second set of practices and disciplines opens us to the living Christ as we embody his life in the ways in which we treat each other and live together. We hold our tongues, learn humility, listen to each other, help each other, bear with each other, and speak God's healing, reproving Word to each other. Bonhoeffer's third set of practices opens us to the living Christ as he is set forth by the sacraments. Confessing our sins, we renew our baptism and come as a reconciled people to the table.

These three categories—Word, ordered life together, and the sacraments—correspond to what the Reformers called the marks of the church. In a world in which the Roman church was fracturing and new church bodies were springing up, the Reformers had to consider how a Christian could distinguish a true church from a false one. Calvin, like Luther, emphasized two criteria: "the Word of God purely preached and heard, and the sacraments administered according to Christ's institution."[28] Calvin emphasized in addition that just "as the saving doctrine of Christ [set forth in the Word proclaimed and the sacraments] is the soul of the church, so does discipline serve as its sinews, through which the members of the body hold together, each in its own place."[29]

Calvin himself did not make discipline a third mark of the church, but several later Reformed confessions (such as the Scots Confession) did. Calvin may have shied away from making discipline a mark because he wanted the church to remain focused on Christ, the living Word, not become obsessed with its own purity. But if we understand church discipline less in terms of church law and church disciplinary proceedings, and more in terms of practices and disciplines of faith, then church discipline bears as much significance as the Word proclaimed and the sacraments.[30] Disciplines of mutual service, like the Word proclaimed and the sacraments, set forth the living Christ. They deepen our identity in him. They draw us into his life.

Baptism represents the beginning of our journey as those on whom God has bestowed an identity. The Lord's Supper represents God's sustenance along the way as well as the heavenly banquet that awaits us at the end. Even now we receive a foretaste of that eternity in which we will be fully identified with Christ and with each other as members of his body. Together with the memory of our baptism and the anticipation of the heavenly feast, practices and disciplines of the Word, life together, and the Eucharist confirm and strengthen our identity as children of the God who is Father, Son, and Holy Spirit.[31]

Chapter Two

Commandments as Identity Markers

> Keep these words that I am commanding you today in your heart. . . . Bind them as a sign on your hand, fix them as an emblem on your forehead, and write them on the doorposts of your house and on your gates.
>
> Deut. 6:6, 8

In the northeastern United States, September 11, 2001, began gloriously. The morning air was cool, the sun warm and bright. In western Pennsylvania the sky was as deep blue as it ever gets. Classes had been in session for only a week; teachers and students alike were basking in the last days of summer. Nothing suggested that this day would become one of the most tragic and ignominious of all days.

I rode my bicycle to the seminary, arriving a few minutes before nine. As I often do, I looked up the day's headlines on the Internet. A brief story about an airplane hitting one of the World Trade Center towers had just been posted. I had no reason to imagine anything more than a small single-engine airplane spinning out of control over the skies of New York—a tragic accident or a suicidal act.

Beginning the day's work, I e-mailed a colleague a piece of business. He immediately e-mailed me back. Had I not heard the terrible news yet? The nation was under attack. I stared at my computer screen—first stunned, then appalled and frightened—as I clicked from one story to the next, trying to make sense of what was happening. For a fleeting moment, I wondered if perhaps the United States had been caught unawares by enemy missiles launched from Russia or China, or even if the world was coming to an end. Soon the first tower collapsed, then the second. Still in front of my computer screen, I broke down in tears. Eventually I phoned my wife, then wandered into the hallway and spoke to a couple of colleagues. But I was paralyzed. I wasn't sure what to do, where to go. I finally made my way home, but not until the end of the day, as though it had been a regular workday. I later wondered why I had not left hours earlier.

I was scheduled to travel to a congregation in Litchfield, Connecticut, on the coming weekend to deliver a theological lecture on a topic that I felt was of concern to the contemporary church. The lecture would take place on Sunday afternoon; the pastor also wanted me to preach on Sunday morning. "More people are more apt to come out to hear you in the afternoon if they have heard you preach in the morning," he explained. On September 12 I phoned the pastor, doubting that the event would still take place. We agreed to wait another day or two. By Thursday afternoon, he had consulted key members of his congregation and decided that I should still come. People wanted scheduled events in the congregation's life to go on as planned.

I agreed to come, but I was uneasy. While I was confident that I could still give my prepared lecture on Sunday afternoon, I was uncertain about what to do on Sunday morning. Should I write a new sermon, directly addressing the events of that week? Should I preach at all? Didn't it make more sense for the pastor himself to preach? Wouldn't his congregation want him in the pulpit? But the pastor insisted that I preach. He assured me that the congregation would want to hear me, their special guest for the day. I could make minor adjustments in the sermon, but he would pick up the concerns of the congregation in other parts of the liturgy, such as the pastoral prayer.

My flight on Saturday afternoon took us out over the ocean, well away from Manhattan. But we could see the smoke still rising from the rubble of the two towers, as the golden sun began to set behind the city. On Sunday, I awoke in the small bed-and-breakfast where the congregation had boarded me and walked to the church, a superb example of New England Congregationalist architecture—a symmetrically arranged, white clapboard meetinghouse, topped by a wooden bell tower and located on the village green in the heart of a quaint town. The interior matched my expectations: wooden pews, a balcony along three walls, and a high central pulpit. Whoever climbed the stairs into the pulpit stood at the level of the balcony and had a commanding view of the entire room.

By eleven o'clock, the meetinghouse was packed. During the service, people wept openly. The pastor conveyed condolences that he had received from a partner congregation in Germany. He then spoke to the children about the tragic events, assuring them that they would be all right, because God would be watching over them. He prayed for the nation, asking for comfort and protection. Finally, I delivered my sermon, doing the best that I knew how to do under the circumstances. I sat, and the service concluded with the hymn, "America."

As we walked to the door to greet people, the pastor thanked me for my words. As members of the congregation filed by, they too were clearly appreciative. But I noticed something: People would greet me and shake my hand, but when they turned to their pastor, they simply looked into his eyes and hugged him, not needing to say a thing. They had an immediate emotional connection with him. On this day of grief, they needed their pastor.

The lecture was still to come. Over lunch, I wondered aloud whether people would return to hear me speak on "The Ten Commandments for the Church Today." Why would anyone want to attend a theological lecture on the commandments, on the Sunday afternoon after 9/11? Attendance was indeed smaller than in previous years, but people did come. They came clearly hoping to hear something that would help them on that difficult weekend. They came not just to be polite, not just to fill seats. Rather, matters of life and death were at stake for them. I had not preached on the commandments that morning; I had not even read them aloud. But what I learned that afternoon persuaded me that I could have.

People wanted to know whether the commandments had something to say to them in their shock and grief. They came, asking themselves, Can we trust that there is a basic moral order to the universe? Can we be confident that our world is not falling into chaos and meaninglessness? Can we be certain that God's ways will prevail? People wanted to know whether the commandments could help them trust again—trust that God was in control, and that God's gracious ordering of the world would hold.

> I am the LORD your God, who brought you out of the land of Egypt, out of the house of slavery; you shall have no other gods before me.
>
> You shall not make for yourself an idol. . . .
>
> You shall not make wrongful use of the name of the LORD your God. . . .

> Remember the sabbath day, and keep it holy. Six days you shall labor and do all your work. But the seventh day is a sabbath to the LORD your God; you shall not do any work—you, your son or your daughter, your male or female slave, your livestock, or the alien resident in your towns. . . .
> Honor your father and your mother. . . .
> You shall not murder.
> You shall not commit adultery.
> You shall not steal.
> You shall not bear false witness against your neighbor.
> You shall not covet. . . . (Exod. 20:1–17)

Commandments of Comfort

As I spoke about the commandments, and as members of the congregation raised questions and offered comments, we together began to understand that the commandments are words of comfort and hope and life. The commandments are more than demands; they are promises. They assure us that God has created humans for good, despite all the evidence that we give to the contrary.

I returned to Pittsburgh with gratitude for the saints in Litchfield. But my experience got me to thinking about what the church says, and how it says it, in times of communal grief. A friend once told me about a time in his ministry when another national tragedy had rendered people speechless and he too had been unsure what and how to preach. He finally decided to throw out the sermon that he had prepared and instead to read and briefly comment on some of the great passages of Scripture to which God's people have turned again and again in times of mourning.

At a time of national tragedy, as at a funeral, the words of Scripture sometimes speak to us more deeply than any of our own words. We just want to hear the familiar, reassuring words of life—the enduring, reliable words in which the church past and present has again and again heard God's Word.

> Have you not known? Have you not heard?
> The LORD is the everlasting God,
>   the Creator of the ends of the earth.
> He does not faint or grow weary;

his understanding is unsearchable.
He gives power to the faint,
and strengthens the powerless.
Even youths will faint and be weary,
and the young will fall exhausted;
but those who wait for the LORD shall renew their strength,
they shall mount up with wings like eagles,
they shall run and not be weary,
they shall walk and not faint.

Isa. 40:28–31

Who will separate us from the love of Christ? Will hardship, or distress, or persecution, or famine, or nakedness, or peril, or sword? As it is written,

"For your sake we are being killed all day long;
we are accounted as sheep to be slaughtered."

No, in all these things we are more than conquerors through him who loved us. For I am convinced that neither death, nor life, nor angels, nor rulers, nor things present, nor things to come, nor powers, nor height, nor depth, nor anything else in all creation, will be able to separate us from the love of God in Christ Jesus our Lord. (Rom. 8:35–39)

Christians turn in their times of trial and tribulation to Scripture. We read the Bible in the confidence that its words will be God's words to us. We go to the Scriptures because we want to know again who we really are. When we stand before the ultimate mysteries of life and death, we long to be reassured that we belong to God and that we bear his triune name. The Scriptures narrate the story that bestows and shapes our core identity. They help us remember God and therefore that we are God's beloved children.

The commandments, too, help us remember. Like Isaiah and Romans, they give us identity markers. They tell us who we really are, because they tell us who God really is—the One who delivers people from the house of bondage. Like the people of Israel, we could profitably bind the commandments to our hands and foreheads, to the doorposts of our houses and our gates. They are words that Christians, like Jews, have always wanted to keep in front of themselves, to guide and direct them in paths of righteousness, and to keep them oriented in times of trial and temptation.

For Christians, the commandments have always been much more than a moral checklist, more than a reason to pat ourselves on the back for our achievements or to hang our heads for our failures. They have described the very character of God and the very character of those who belong to God.[1] The first table—no other gods, no idols, no wrongful use of God's name, and keeping Sabbath—should characterize our relationship with God. The second table—honoring father and mother, not killing, not committing adultery, not stealing, not bearing false witness, and not coveting—should characterize our relationships with each other. Together the commandments remind us of the basic moral order that God has established and that marks all human beings at their core.

God's Good Order for Humanity

Every human being? People today are apt to think of the commandments as part of the Judeo-Christian tradition, not as self-evident truths that every person in the world unquestionably accepts as marks of his or her humanity. The commandments do, of course, belong especially to Jews and Christians. They have deeply marked the religious heritage of the West. But to call the commandments Judeo-Christian is to say both too much and too little. It is to say too much because these "ten words" (Decalogue) have never played the central role in Judaism that they have in Christianity. Jews have spoken more broadly of the Torah (God's instruction) and also more specifically of the 613 requirements of the Torah. They have not wanted to suggest that God's will for Israel could be reduced to the Ten Commandments.

It is also to say too *little*. Early Christians (and some Jews, such as the first-century philosopher Philo) insisted that the commandments had universal import, representing not just obligations for the church (or Israel), but for all humanity. The commandments said something about the deepest identity of every person. They offered a picture of human life together as God meant it to be—as it once characterized paradise and as it should one day find fulfillment in the new heaven and the new earth of which the book of Revelation speaks.

Early Christians believed that the Decalogue corresponded to what philosophers of the day called "natural law," the idea that in creating the world, God had inscribed a rational order into it. As the apostle Paul had noted:

> Ever since the creation of the world [God's] eternal power and divine nature, invisible though they are, have been understood and seen through the things he has made. (Rom. 1:20)
>
> When Gentiles, who do not possess the law [that is, the law revealed to Israel], do instinctively what the law requires, these, though not having the law, are a law to themselves. They show that what the law requires is written on their hearts, to which their own conscience also bears witness; and their conflicting thoughts will accuse or perhaps excuse them on the day when, according to my gospel, God, through Jesus Christ, will judge the secret thoughts of all. (Rom. 2:14–16)

Natural law theology taught that God had created the world to show forth his nature and will. Humans through their reason could discern this divine order and the divine Orderer behind it. In addition, God had given humans a conscience that confronted them with a fundamental moral order within themselves that corresponded to the natural order of the world.

Early Christians believed that the God whom humans knew through natural law and their conscience was the same God whom Christians knew in Jesus Christ. Christ, they claimed, did not appear for the first time in the historical man Jesus of Nazareth; rather, as the second person of the Trinity, he had existed from before the beginning of time. He was the Logos, or the Word (better translated perhaps as "the Reason" or "the Order"). All who understood the world and its natural order were somehow already coming to know the Son of God. The Bible again, especially the opening lines of the Gospel of John, stimulated this line of thinking: "In the beginning was the Word [Logos]. . . . All things came into being through him. . . . In him was life, and the life was the light of all people. . . . The true light, which enlightens everyone, was coming into the world" (John 1:1, 3, 4, 9). Christ, the Logos, seemed to reside in every human being, offering every human being light and life and order.

Drawing on these ideas, the Christian thinker Justin argued, only a century after Jesus' death, that "Christ is the First-begotten of God. . . .

He is the Reason [Logos] of which every man partakes. Those who live in accordance with Reason are Christians, even though they were called godless."[2] Human reason is not merely the ability to think logically but is a participation in the very character of God. We are marked—by nature, by reason, by conscience, and ultimately by Christ himself—to live according to the fundamental moral order that God has established. The commandments set forth God's intentions for all humanity, not just Jews and Christians. They describe reality more truly than any of our great science or literature, philosophy or mathematics.

The Christian tradition has struggled with the fact that humans, nevertheless, do not live consistently by their God-given reason or their natural knowledge of God but, rather, regularly depart from the moral order that God has established, denying their true selves. Instead of leading men and women to the divine Reason, human reason inevitably becomes calculating and self-serving. Thus, human conscience is no longer a reliable guide to the things of God. We easily find ourselves feeling guilty about things that we should not, and not guilty about things that we should. Paul himself raised questions about how far the natural law can guide us under the conditions of sin. All it now does, he suggests, is to leave us "without excuse" (Rom. 1:20). It accuses us but cannot direct us aright. The natural law is inscribed on our hearts and is our true character, yet it turns out that we are now unable to live by it.

Ever since Paul, Christians have debated to just what extent natural law and natural knowledge of God have been obscured. Does sin hold the conscience entirely captive? Has human reason lost all ability to discern the good? Different parts of the Christian tradition have answered differently, especially at the time of the Reformation. The Reformers believed that medieval Catholic theology had shown too much confidence in reason. They argued that humans had largely lost their capacity to discern the natural law and live by it. God has marked us as his, but we rebel, wanting to be something else. Somewhere deep in our hearts we may vaguely know that we are made to worship the true God, but we turn instead to gods of our own making. We may know that we are made to care for each other, but we inevitably look out for ourselves first and neglect and even harm others.

Christians of different traditions, Catholic and Protestant, have nevertheless agreed that some spark of God's goodness remains in humanity, despite our capacity to distort the good. Even in a sinful world, societies continue to be concerned to establish justice, and human beings continue to have an intrinsic sense of right and wrong. By nature, people continue to know, for instance, that killing and adultery and stealing are wrong, even though different societies and individuals vary widely both in how they define these activities and in what exceptions they allow.

The natural capacity to know the good may never be absent altogether, but it is very fragile. If humans are to recognize the good and live by it, we need help. Early Christians believed that God had revealed the Ten Commandments to Israel for just that reason. The commandments called God's people back to the natural law inscribed on their hearts. The commandments helped people to recover their sight—to see God's will clearly again.

Following this line of thought, Christians have noted that the commandments really do not tell us anything that we do not already know. They simply clarify what ought to be self-evident truths about killing, adultery, and stealing. We should have no problem recognizing that violating the commandments makes it more difficult for people to live together and violates the very person who commits this violation, diminishing his or her humanity.

Yet Christians have also asserted that we now need the commandments more than ever. Apparently, they are not so self-evident. Humans continue to kill, commit adultery, and steal, even after centuries of living with the negative repercussions. We need the commandments to stand over and against us as stark reminders of the God-given identity that we would rather neglect or forget. We need them in order to confront the truth about ourselves, namely, that God did not create us to kill or commit adultery or steal.

As we have seen, many Jews and Christians of the past would have added that humans are also made naturally for relationship with God—and not just an abstract, indeterminate God of transcendence, but the God who makes covenant with Israel and a new covenant with the church. Again, these Jews and Christians believed that none of the Ten Commandments tell us anything different from what our reason and common sense should already tell us—namely, that we have been made to worship the true God and to serve one another in accordance with God's will. Both tables of the law point us to our true life in God.

Commandments and the Civil Law

Because the commandments have universal import, Christians (who more than Jews have held political power in Western European history) have sometimes argued that the commandments provide the moral foundations for civil government, that righteous government will base its laws on the natural law to which the commandments correspond. Especially up through the Middle Ages and the Reformation, many Christians insisted that the state had the responsibility to enforce both the commandments about right worship of God and the commandments about right relationship among human beings. The French Confession of 1559, influenced by Calvin, is typical:

> We believe that God wills the world to be governed by laws and policies that provide restraints on disordered worldly appetites. Therefore, God has established kingdoms and republics and all other sorts of principalities, hereditary or otherwise, as well as everything pertaining to the state of justice. Because God wills to be recognized as their author he has placed the sword in the hands of the civil authorities to suppress sins committed against the first table of the Law as well as the second. For God's sake, then, we must not only submit to the authority of superiors but also respect and honor them as God's deputies and officials, commissioned to exercise a legitimate and holy charge.[3]

Even today, Christians can recognize a kernel of truth in this position. Historians have noted that the emergence of political democracies in the West depended on the moral foundations of the Jewish and Christian traditions.[4] Both tables of the Decalogue were important to the democratic experiment. The first table set limitations on the state's power; the second table taught the state its responsibilities to its citizens. Contemporary defenders of the political relevance of the Decalogue remind us of the mural in the chambers of the United States Supreme Court that depicts Moses holding the Ten Commandments, and they note that government buildings in the United States have often posted the commandments. Some of these defenders of the Decalogue actively resist efforts to remove the commandments from the public sphere.[5]

But few of us—and even few of those who defend public posting of the commandments—would argue that the state should enforce all the commandments. Christians may believe that God has marked every human being in his image. We may hope for a world in which every knee shall bow and every tongue confess that Jesus Christ is Lord. But most of us would agree that people discover their identity in Christ only through the gift of faith, not through state coercion. We want a state that will make room for the church to proclaim the commandments, but we are not interested in religious inquisition and intolerance and strife.

Nevertheless, Christians and non-Christians alike have reason to ask the government to enforce at least some of what the commandments prescribe. When it comes to matters of killing and stealing, we want the state to take charge. (Thanks be to God for righteous police officers and courts!) But the state's role in other areas of the commandments is often less than desirable. The question of adultery is illustrative. While the state remains rightly concerned about regulating aspects of marriage, few of us want the state to impose legal penalties on the adulterer. The human complexities are too great. We hope that the adulterer receives counseling. We wish to ensure the economic protection of the abandoned spouse. But we rightfully doubt the effectiveness of laws against adultery. Christians know that they cannot force people to be faithful to God, and Christians legitimately question whether the state can force spouses to be faithful to each other.

What is true about adultery applies to the other commandments as well. Is it the state's business to enforce a day of rest, or is Sabbath keeping a matter of personal persuasion? We likely welcome laws that regulate hours of employment but not a return to blue laws. What kinds of lying should the state guard against? We probably want legal protection in contracts, but no state-imposed penalties for the everyday white lies that we tell each other, as destructive as they can be.

The first table and its commandments regarding right worship raise particularly challenging questions. As we have noted, the Christian tradition long insisted that rulers should enforce right belief. Yet as Western democracies have evolved, they have seen the wisdom of separating church and state. The state should mostly stay out of matters of religious belief. Historical experience has taught that when the state sponsors religion or combats heresy, great harm ultimately results not only to society but also to the church itself. A state that regulates religious belief threatens to become totalitarian and to assume powers that belong to God alone.

The state's relationship to the first table has another side, however. From a Christian perspective, a state that refrains from enforcing the first table should nevertheless make space for freedom of religious expression. The state must not promote a particular religion or coerce religious belief, but it should acknowledge that religious belief encourages people to be more responsible citizens—to care for others, to speak truthfully, and to conduct affairs honestly—and therefore contributes to the vitality of a democratic society.[6] Christians will argue that the state should continue to be concerned about the first table because the first table underlies the second—that is to say, morality can be firmly grounded only in belief in a God who watches over us and calls us to account.

Christians therefore have reason even today to ask the state to attend to *all* of the Ten Commandments and to the order of things that *both* tables set forth. We will remind the state that the commandments point not only to *Christian* identity but also to *human* identity—what it means to be truly human. Here again, however, difficult questions arise: Just how should Christians represent the humanitarian vision of the commandments to a secular state? For a secular state is apt to see the Ten Commandments only as sectarian, belonging to a particular religious tradition. It will not want to base itself explicitly on the commandments, even if it has a legitimate concern for many of the areas of life that the commandments identify.

Christians need not insist that the state become Christian, but they will remind even a secular state that humanity's God-given identity is more fundamental than its national identities. Similarly, Christians need not insist that the Ten Commandments be posted on government buildings, but they will insist that the state is responsible to maintain a basic civil order in which people can freely conform their lives to what Christians believe is a person's truest self—a self that worships God and serves others. In the interest of social stability, the state should provide for a minimal expression of the commandments.

At the same time, Christians will never rest content with merely stating the civic implications of the Decalogue, for the commandments ask Christians to be concerned not only with the minimum that we should expect of the state but also with the maximum that God requires of believers. The commandments ultimately summon Christians to a way of life that cannot be mandated by the state but that becomes possible only by God's intervening grace. In the end, influencing the state is only one limited means by which Christians set forth the truth that they find in the commandments. More significantly, Christians attend to the commandments because they lead them to Jesus Christ and the new life that he alone makes possible—the new life that confirms our God-given baptismal identity.

We will thus truly live by the commandments only if they become more than a social expectation. They must shape us from the inside out.

They must become internal principles of action, not simply external legal demands. They must become nothing less than our second nature. Christians will always remember that the state cannot give us our true humanity; only God can. The commandments are for all humanity, and all humanity ultimately depends on the grace of God for its redemption.

Deepening the Commandments

I have argued up to now that the Ten Commandments offer humans comfort. They assure us that God has created us to correspond to the order that he has established. They remind us that we are most truly ourselves when we live in the way that the commandments describe. When the world outside us or inside us seems to be falling apart, the commandments remind us of a deeper reality. Despite all the evidence in the world to the contrary, the commandments assure us that God's order will prevail.

Too often, however, the comfort that we find in the commandments is false. We use them as a moral checklist. We look at them and congratulate ourselves on how well we have done:

> "No other gods before me." Fine, I'm a Christian.
> "No graven images." No problems with that one either.
> "Do not take the name of the Lord your God in vain." We assure ourselves that we did not say any curse words today.
> "Keep the Sabbath day holy." Did we go to church? Did we stay away from the office?

Having cycled our way through the first table, we begin the second. "Honor your father and mother." We are sure that we do our best. "Do not kill." Most of us can say that we have never committed murder. "Do not commit adultery." Most of us (but perhaps fewer) can get to the end of the day and say, No problem there. Most of us (but perhaps even fewer) will have complied with "Do not steal." By the time we get to lying and coveting, we may squirm. Still, we find comfort in believing that we have lived up to the commandments fairly well.

At its best, the Christian tradition has rejected this false comfort. It has insisted, instead, that the commandments make a total demand on us, that they set forth God's claim on every area of our lives and describe a way of life that is nothing less than life in and with God. To explicate the comprehensive meaning of the commandments, Christian interpreters, especially during the Middle Ages and the Reformation, typically made three interpretive moves, each of which has continuing relevance for the church.[7]

First, these interpreters *broadened* each commandment so that it represents a category of behaviors, not a single behavior. "Do not kill" is only the most vivid, heinous crime in a category that could be called, "Do not harm your neighbor." Killing is not only a specific physical act. We can kill with our words. We can cut people off emotionally. We can neglect others. Calvin once said that God says, "Do not kill," in order to get our attention. Once God gets our attention, we may say to ourselves, "Well, I don't kill." But soon we find ourselves having to think about other ways in which we hurt others.[8]

Second, the Decalogue's interpreters *internalized* each commandment, understanding it to refer not only to external actions but also to internal attitudes and motivations. "No other gods before me" and "no graven images" refer as much to where we place our ultimate trust and loyalty as they do to sculpted idols of wood or stone. "Do not steal" is not only about taking property that does not belong to us but is also about desiring what is not ours. This internal dimension of the commandments is also suggested by the tenth, "Do not covet." Wrong desire underlies every violation of the commandments, just as right desire upholds them.

Third, Christian interpreters have typically explicated the full meaning of each commandment by *reversing* it. They have argued that each positive implies a negative, each negative a positive. The Sabbath commandment states both a positive and a negative: Keep this day holy, do no work. The other commandments imply similar reversals. "Do not take the name of the Lord your God in vain" also means, "Speak rightly about God and God's purposes." "Do not kill" implies "Do everything that you can to promote life." "Do not commit adultery" includes the commitment to "do everything that you can to live with integrity in your relationships, especially marriage."

When the commandments are explicated in this way, none of us can get to the end of the day and conclude that we're okay. All of us fall short. None of us measures up. For this reason, Christians have often used the Ten Commandments to evoke and guide their confession of sin. In the sixteenth century, the Anglican Book of Common Prayer prescribed that the priest read the commandments immediately after the opening acts of worship. After each commandment, the people were to respond, "Lord, have mercy upon us, and incline our hearts to keep thy law."[9] Similarly, Bonhoeffer recommended that his seminarians use the commandments to examine themselves and confess their sins before God and each other.[10]

From this perspective, the commandments offer us comfort only to the extent that they direct us to God's forgiveness. The accusing law drives us to Christ's mercy. Our comfort is not in the commandments but in the One who has fulfilled them on our behalf. When we explicate their meaning in full, we only see how far we still have to go. We feel guilt and shame that we are not yet the people God created us to be.

Commandments and Love

But isn't love—God's love—rather than the commandments, the center of the Christian gospel? The Heidelberg Catechism of 1562 in its opening lines defines the Christian life in this way: "What is your only comfort, in life and in death? That I belong—body and soul, in life and in death—not to myself but to my faithful Savior, Jesus Christ, who at the cost of his own blood has fully paid for all my sins and has completely freed me from the dominion of the devil" (q. 1). The catechism does not refer us to the Ten Commandments but to God's mercy in Jesus Christ. In Christ, we are free of the accusing law. In Christ, we have sure salvation. In Christ, we can claim the great promises of Isaiah and Romans, that no matter what we have done, no matter what has befallen us, God loves us and will not let us go. We don't need the commandments—or do we?

There is no doubt that the confession "God is love" goes to the very heart of the biblical witness. For Christians, this witness reaches its high point in God's gracious acts in Jesus Christ: "God so loved the world that he gave his only Son" (John 3:16). "God's love was revealed among us in this way: God sent his only Son into the world so that we might live through him" (1 John 4:9). Scripture reminds Christians of a love so amazing, so divine, that God himself meets them in the life, death, and resurrection of Jesus Christ. Moreover, this comforting love transforms us. In Christ, we are a new creation: "Everything old has passed away; see, everything has become new!" (2 Cor. 5:17). We have died with Christ so that we might be raised to new life with him. We no longer live for ourselves, but for God and others:

> We know that our old self was crucified with him so that the body of sin might be destroyed. . . . But if we have died with Christ, we believe that we will also live with him. (Rom. 6:6, 8)

> God, who is rich in mercy, out of the great love with which he loved us even when we were dead through our trespasses, made us alive together with Christ—by grace you have been saved—and raised us up with him. (Eph. 2:4–6)

As those who belong to Christ, we now participate in his self-renouncing, self-giving love.

Here we suddenly see that God's love not only comforts but also demands, not only accepts us but also reshapes us. God's love does not let us off the hook but challenges us to be a different kind of people. God's love touches us to the quick and redirects us. God is love, and those whom God has claimed in Christ share in this love: "Beloved, let us love one another, because love is from God; everyone who loves is born of God and knows God" (1 John 4:7). God asks us to love in the way that Christ has loved. As the apostle Paul puts it,

> Let the same mind be in you that was in Christ Jesus,
> who, though he was in the form of God,
>   did not regard equality with God
>   as something to be exploited,
> but emptied himself,
>   taking the form of a slave,
>   being born in human likeness.
> And being found in human form,
>   he humbled himself
>   and became obedient to the point of death—
>   even death on a cross.
>
> Phil. 2:5–8

If there is "any consolation from love" (Phil. 2:1), it now derives not only from what God has done for us in Christ but also from what we have become in Christ: a new self, shaped by and for God's love.

Christ has set us apart for a life of love, and love is the principal mark of our identity in him. But now another question presents itself: Just what does it mean to love? What does it mean to love God, who is Spirit? We know how to make gods of our own choosing. We know how to love power and wealth and pleasure. But how do we come to know and love the God who is the maker of heaven and earth, and therefore the very source of our being?

We should love, as Christ loved. But what does it mean to love our neighbors, when we are never able to get out of our own skin into theirs? We know that we should try to do unto others as we would have them do unto us, but we inevitably skew our relations with them in favor of our own perspective and our own self-interest. As one contemporary confession of faith puts it, "All human virtue, when seen in the light of God's love in Jesus Christ, is found to be infected by self-interest and hostility."[11]

If we are to love in the way that God loves (and so resisting our sinful tendency to define love in our own terms), we must identify and describe love's contours as carefully as possible. What, if anything, is distinctive about the love that we encounter in Christ? What does Christ's love require in one specific situation or another? Just how do we love in the way that Christ loved?

To know this love, Christians over the centuries have turned first of all to Scripture. They have remembered the words of Jesus, how in his Sermon on the Mount and elsewhere he commended meekness and mercy and peaceableness. Surely the new life of love looked something like the life of those of whom Jesus spoke in his Beatitudes.

In examining Scripture, Christians have also looked to the example of Jesus, remembering how he ate with tax collectors, cast out demons, healed a paralyzed man and a hemorrhaging woman, and blessed his enemies. Christians have concluded that the love of Jesus surely meant a radical concern for the good of others, even at the expense of one's self.

Moreover, Christians have noted that Christian love is more than a fleeting feeling, more than a romantic outburst of well-being. It has not been something that one simply fell in or out of. Rather, Christian love has implied a reorienting of one's whole existence, a reshaping of one's deepest motivations. One has to become a new self. The apostle Paul identifies key dispositions or affections that characterize this new self, insofar as it is given to love. Paul speaks first of fruit of the Spirit: "love, joy, peace, patience, kindness, generosity, faithfulness, gentleness, and self-control" (Gal. 5:22–23). He adds that we are "to lead a life worthy of the calling to which [we] have been called, with all humility and gentleness, with patience, bearing with one another in love" (Eph. 4:1–2). He also speaks of "compassion, kindness, humility, meekness, and patience" (Col. 3:12). The Christian has a new inner core that guides and directs everything that he or she does.

Christians have also turned to the Ten Commandments to understand more fully the character of Christian love and the fruit of the Spirit. As we have noted, the Ten Commandments at first glance do not seem to tell us much about this love or this new inner core. As a result, the Christian tradition has sometimes set law and grace in opposition to each other—the commandments on one side, and the life of Christian love on the other. Old Testament law has then been regarded as part of the old life from which Christians have been freed. No longer need they obey the requirements of the old covenant; no longer do they seek a righteousness based on their own works. The apostle Paul argues that we are "justified by faith apart from works prescribed by the law" (Rom. 3:28). "The law was our disciplinarian until Christ came, so that we might be justified by faith. But now that faith has come, we are no longer subject to a disciplinarian" (Gal. 3:24–25). But to end Christian theology on an antilegalistic note would be too shortsighted.

Christian love does spring forth freely and spontaneously from our new being in Christ.[12] God's love does flow through us. But the new life in Christ also has structure and order. God's love runs deep in predictable channels. Paul rejects the law, only to speak of the law of Christ (Gal. 6:2). Likewise, the author of the First Letter of John reminds us that law and grace, commandment and love, do not contradict but support each other:

> Now by this we may be sure that we know him, if we obey his commandments. Whoever says, "I have come to know him," but does not obey his commandments, is a liar, and in such a person the truth does not exist; but whoever obeys his word, truly in this person the love of God has reached perfection. (1 John 2:3–5)

> And this is his commandment, that we should believe in the name of his Son Jesus Christ and love one another, just as he has commanded us. All who obey his commandments abide in him, and he abides in them. (1 John 3:23–24)

> By this we know that we love the children of God, when we love God and obey his commandments. For the love of God is this, that we obey his commandments. And his commandments are not burdensome. (1 John 5:2–3)

From this perspective, the commandments, as valuable as they are, are more than a minimalist program for a stable civil order. But they are also more than an accusing finger that keeps scolding us about how far short we fall of the perfect life that is God's. Rather, the commandments mark the new life in Christ that is truly ours, here and now. They tell us who we really are and therefore what we are really capable of doing as people who belong to Jesus Christ. Bonhoeffer's words about the Sermon on the Mount apply equally well to the commandments: "'You *are* the salt'—not 'you should be the salt'! . . . [The disciples] just are salt, whether they want to be or not, by the power of the call that has reached them. . . . 'You *are* the light'—again, not: 'you should be the light'!"[13]

What does the life of Christian love look like? What does it mean for Christians to be salt and light and love? Simply this—to walk in the way of the commandments. Have no other gods, but love the Lord your God with all your heart, and all your soul, and all your mind. Do not kill or commit adultery or steal, but love your neighbor as yourself. Let each commandment lead you along a concrete, specific moral trajectory of love that declares, "Here is the right direction in which to go if you want to grow in the Christian life." We need not despair that the commandments as broadened, internalized, and reversed are only an impossible, unreachable standard. Rather, the commandments show us how we can grow more fully into the stature of Jesus Christ.

Those churches that at the time of the Reformation came to be known as Reformed (because they wanted to reform all church life according to God's Word) acknowledged the civil and accusatory uses of the law but particularly emphasized its "third use." In this third use, the law "finds its place among believers in whose heart the Spirit of God already lives and reigns."[14] It teaches and exhorts, arouses and directs. It spurs us to live and love in the way of Christ, in whom by virtue of our baptism we now have our true identity. As Calvin notes,

> However eagerly [the saints] may in accordance with the Spirit strive toward God's righteousness, the listless flesh always so burdens them that they do not proceed with due readiness. The law is to the flesh like a whip to an idle and balky ass, to arouse it to work. Even for a spiritual man not yet free of the weight of the flesh the law remains a constant sting that will not let him stand still. . . . But the accompanying promise of grace . . . sweetens what is bitter.[15]

The commandments do not cease to make demands, even on Christians. But these demands now come as much from within as from without. No longer do the commandments simply stand over and against us. Rather, they lie at our inner core. They set forth the way of life that Christ has made possible for us. They tell us what we now want to do (in the words of Karl Barth, the greatest Protestant theologian of the twentieth century, what we are now *permitted* to do), so that we may grow in faithfulness to the One who has been faithful to us.[16]

Each commandment suggests a set of practices and disciplines that reshape Christians' lives, individually and corporately. Each commandment suggests a way of life into which we grow with others and by ourselves over a lifetime. "Have no other gods before me" becomes the daily practice of keeping our focus on God when other things compete for our attention. "Do not kill" becomes the daily practice of promoting others' good, even at expense to oneself. "Do not commit adultery," "Do not steal," "Do not bear false witness"—each becomes a discipline of love, at which we must work again and again.

As such, we can never simply choose whether or not to obey the commandments, for we cannot practice them on our own initiative or under our own power but only as we are led by the Holy Spirit, the giver of life—and the giver of new life in Christ. The commandments help describe the trajectories along which the Spirit works. The practices and disciplines of the commandments are avenues along which the Spirit moves, bringing us into deeper fellowship with God and with each other. Each commandment offers a pathway of freedom into life in Christ.[17]

As contributing to our sanctification—that is, our growth into God's righteousness and holiness—the commandments mark Christians as *Christians*. As we have noted, rather than simply representing the minimalist demands of a just social order, they point us to the maximalist demands of life in Christ and so have specifically Christian meaning. Nevertheless, they also have continuing significance for humanity as a whole. We return to where we began: with the assertion that the commandments mark out not only a Christian but also a *human* identity.

God will not simply save Israel or the church as a faithful remnant, while condemning the rest of the world. God has called both Israel and the church—each in its own way, yet neither without the other—to represent God's will for all humanity: "I will give you as a light to the nations, that my salvation may reach to the end of the earth" (Isa. 49:6). "Nations shall come to your light, and kings to the brightness of your dawn" (Isa. 60:3). "You are the light of the world. A city built on a hill cannot be hid" (Matt. 5:14). "I saw the holy city, the new Jerusalem. . . . The nations will walk by its light" (Rev. 21:2, 24). The Ten Commandments have special import for the church, but they are also light for the world. They illuminate what every human life is about.

The church casts this light into the world whenever it proclaims to society the humanitarian vision of the commandments and whenever it works in society for the realization of this humanitarian vision.[18] But the church casts light above all when it embodies the commandments in its own way of life. A Christian community that practices the commandments is already salt and light and love. It offers the world comfort and hope and life, because it says, "Look, here you can see, however imperfectly and incompletely, a small reflection of the way of life that God has inscribed on the heart of every human being."[19] Theologians have sometimes expressed this point by calling the church to be the provisional representation of God's kingdom—a huge task, a task at which the church will surely fail, but nevertheless a task of profound importance. To be the church is to be light to the nations, inviting the whole world to know the way of the commandments—the way of life before the one true God.

Commandments and Thanksgiving

In a chaotic, disorienting world, the commandments help us keep our focus on God. By guiding us into God's love, they offer us strength for the journey ahead. When we walk in the ways of the commandments, we become more like Christ and therefore more like God himself. In this sense, the commandments do offer us comfort—more, indeed, than we could ever expect.

Life under the commandments is a life of practice and discipline. We will never exhaust the commandments' possibilities. At the end of the day, we will see that we always have more to do. But we do this work gladly and gratefully, because it permits us to lay claim more fully to the selves that God has created us to be. Therein lies great, great comfort, a comfort that the Reformed tradition has vividly illustrated, on behalf of the entire Christian tradition, in the Heidelberg Catechism, the ordering of Lord's Day worship, and church architecture.

The Ten Commandments in the Heidelberg Catechism

After assuring us that our only comfort is in Christ, the Heidelberg Catechism divides into three parts. The first part establishes "Man's Misery." The second reminds us of "Man's Redemption." The third section, entitled "Thankfulness," directs us to how we live out the redeemed life—that is, the life of Christian love. The catechism's discussion of the

Ten Commandments does not appear under "man's misery," even though we have seen that the commandments do accuse us. Nor does it come under "man's redemption," for only the Son's work of obedience can save us, not our own. Rather, the catechism discusses the commandments under "Thankfulness," at the climax of the catechism. The commandments guide us into the gracious way of life that Christ has made possible for us: "Just as Christ has redeemed us with his blood he also renews us through his Holy Spirit according to his own image, so that with our whole life [in obedience to the commandments!] we may show ourselves grateful to God for his goodness and that he may be glorified through us" (q. 86).

The Ten Commandments in Reformed Worship

Before moving to Geneva, Calvin lived in Strasbourg, where he worked closely with the Reformer Martin Bucer. Under Bucer's influence, Calvin developed an order of worship that included a recitation of the Ten Commandments. But he did not use the commandments to evoke confession, in contrast to what the Anglican Book of Common Prayer later did. Instead, he placed the commandments *after* the confession of sin and the assurance of pardon. And instead of Calvin reading them to the people, they said the commandments together as their grateful response to God's mercy. Finally, the people did not simply *say* the words; they *sang* the commandments. They lifted up their voices in praise for God's great gift of the law.[20]

The Reformed tradition has never had any problem joining the psalmist in proclaiming,

> Oh, how I love thy law!
> It is my meditation all the day.
> . . .
> How sweet are thy words to my taste,
> sweeter than honey to my mouth!
> Through thy precepts I get understanding;
> therefore I hate every false way.
> Thy word is a lamp to my feet
> and a light to my path.
> Ps. 119:97, 103–5 RSV

The commandments are God's merciful gift to God's covenant people.

The Ten Commandments in Church Art

The Reformers wanted to emphasize that Christians had their identity in Christ alone. Worship was to help them rehearse this identity. As they heard the Word proclaimed, participated in the sacraments, and ordered their lives together, they could be confident that they were encountering God's living presence in Christ. As they responded in joy and thanksgiving, confession and recommitment, they could be certain that they were growing more fully into the new life in Christ.

The Reformed tradition saw Word, sacrament, and disciplined life in Christian community as moments of covenant making between God and his people. Nothing should distract from the centrality of these three chief identity markers of the church's life in Christ—not adoration of Mary and the saints, not elaborate liturgical rituals, not the privileges of a hierarchical clergy. For this reason, Reformed churches in places such as Scotland, the Netherlands, and Switzerland purged their sanctuaries of liturgical distractions. They tore out ornate medieval and Renaissance altars, removed statues of the saints, and covered ancient wall paintings with whitewash. What remained for the people to see was only that which represented Word, sacrament, and disciplined life together: the pulpit from which the Scriptures were read and proclaimed (the Word), the table at which the community gathered to remember its baptismal identity and to be strengthened in that identity by the Eucharist (sacrament), and, frequently on a side wall, a wooden tablet with the words of the Ten Commandments, directing people to their responsibilities to God and to each other (disciplined life together).[21]

Each commandment represented a major category or area of the Christian life. In their explications of Scripture, Reformed theologians frequently organized biblical materials to fit under one commandment or another; all of Scripture's heroes and villains, divine injunctions, and moral examples helped to illustrate the Decalogue's trajectories. Taken together, the commandments represented a compendium of the Christian life. They directed Christians in practices and disciplines of right worship and right service: "This is who you are. Go, and live it out."

Did people feel guilty every time they looked at a Decalogue plaque? Or did they remember the God who had been so merciful as to guide them into paths of righteousness for his name's sake? Whatever they saw, the commandments were now the marks of their life, the life that Christ in his mercy was making possible. Worshipers could be grateful and raise their voices in praise, perhaps in words like these: “Now to him who by the power at work within us is able to accomplish abundantly far more than all we can ask or imagine, to him be glory in the church and in Christ Jesus to all generations, forever and ever. Amen” (Eph. 3:20–21).

Chapter Three

Free Zones

> Remember the sabbath day, and keep it holy. Six days you shall labor and do all your work. But the seventh day is a sabbath to the LORD your God; you shall not do any work.
>
> Exod. 20:8–10

In 1996, I was an ecumenical delegate to the German Kirchentag, a biannual Protestant church congress that attracts 100,000 people or more to a week of concerts, lectures, workshops, and displays, housed in exhibition halls, as well as many churches. The Kirchentag was held that year in Hamburg, and Hamburg was of special interest to me because it was the home of some of my ancestors. My background is primarily English and Scottish, and I come from a long line of Presbyterian ministers, but I also have these German ancestors, and they were Jewish. One branch of my Jewish family achieved a degree of historical fame, the Heines (including Heinrich Heine, the great Romantic poet), although I am more directly related to the Hertzes, one of whom married a Heine. I had long heard the Heine and Hertz names from my father, and a cousin had prepared a genealogical chart on which she had been able to locate many of them by name and date of birth and death.

I had been too busy at the Kirchentag to do any genealogical investigating, but one afternoon I unexpectedly came across traces of my family history. Walking through an exhibition hall, I paused at a book display and noticed a book about famous cemeteries in Hamburg. To my surprise, the index contained several references for Heine and Hertz, including coordinates for grave locations. I jotted them down and resolved to find them before I left Hamburg.

I was flying home on Sunday. On Saturday morning, I rode the subway to the cemetery, some ten or fifteen miles outside the city center. The grounds were massive, with tens of thousands of graves. But every row was clearly marked, most of the gravesites were identified by coordinates, and eventually I found the Hertz family plot. To my great disappointment, however, none of the names on the tombstones matched the names of my ancestors. Perhaps it was a different set of Hertzes—I could not be sure. I still had time to track down the one Heine grave to which the cemeteries book had referred. It belonged to Solomon, a wealthy, influential banker of the early nineteenth century, uncle of the poet Heinrich, and business partner of Levin Hertz (my direct ancestor). Of all my Jewish ancestors, Solomon interested me most because of a family story that had been passed down about him.

Civic leaders in Hamburg used to call on Solomon regularly, asking for advice or financial contributions to one cause or another. One day, two men from a local Protestant parish visited. Their church had burned to the ground, and they were trying to raise money for a new building. Somewhat hesitatingly, they asked Solomon the Jew whether he would be willing to contribute. Solomon wrote out a check and handed it to them. They thanked him, left the bank, and only then looked at the check. They were astonished by the amount—it was by far the largest donation that they had received. It was so large in fact that they were embarrassed. Surely it couldn't be right. They walked back to the bank and awkwardly returned the check to Solomon, saying that there must have been a mistake. Solomon examined the check and exclaimed, "You are quite right, gentlemen." With that, he proceeded to add another zero, handed them the check again, and wished them a good day.

As I searched for Solomon's grave that day, I discovered that it did not lie in the main cemetery but in a much smaller Jewish cemetery that bordered it, a ten-minute walk away. When I arrived, however, its high metal gates were padlocked. Jewish cemeteries are not open on the Sabbath. My plans had been thwarted. There was nothing to do but return home.

Five years later, I was on the trail of Solomon Heine again. I had been invited to visit the Protestant theological faculty in Prague. My family accompanied me, and we decided that after the two weeks in the Czech Republic, we would spend the rest of the summer, nearly three months, in eastern Germany, an area that we knew well. In late July, we found ourselves in Berlin and decided to take a short side trip to Hamburg. We arrived by train, grabbed the subway, and found the house where we would stay with friends of friends.

My wife and girls and I immediately went to work, for we had only forty-eight hours. On the first day, we learned that many of the sites associated with Jewish life in Hamburg had been destroyed by a massive fire in 1848 or by the Second World War. Solomon's house in the center of Hamburg was gone, as was his bank. But we did find the site of his country estate, now in a suburban area of the city, with a beautiful view of the Hamburg harbor. Old, gnarled trees and the gardener's house, recently restored, were the last tangible signs of Solomon's times.

On the second day, we journeyed to the gates of the Jewish cemetery where I had stood five years earlier. This time they were open. Unfortunately, I no longer had the coordinates for the gravesite. I would have to inquire at the cemetery office. But bad luck struck again. The office was closed, and we saw no one at all on the cemetery grounds. Eventually, we walked to the back of the cemetery, where we discovered some old tombstones that had been moved from other Jewish cemeteries. Most were written in faded Hebrew letters, and I no longer remembered enough from my seminary days to decipher them. A few gravestones, however, were written in German, including that of Betty Heine, Heinrich's mother. We hoped that Solomon's was nearby. Yet again, no luck.

Near the cemetery entrance was a large shed. Music blared from a radio, and a car was parked nearby. No one was in sight, but I finally screwed up my courage and called out. I got no response, but after several minutes two men suddenly appeared—cemetery workers. I told them my problem. They just shook their heads no. I continued to plead, and one finally agreed to help. He took me to the office, unlocked the door, and opened the card catalog. To my relief, Solomon's gravesite was listed. Finally, I had the coordinates.

Time was now getting tight. In an hour, we would have to return to the city to catch a train out of town. Much of the cemetery was overgrown; we made our way through weeds and small trees that had sprung up between the tombstones. Eventually, we came into a newer part of the cemetery—and suddenly we stood before a new, simple, marble stone. Nothing was inscribed on it other than the names of Solomon and his wife (another Betty). The plot was clean and neatly planted. We bowed, as though in prayer, took a couple of photos, and hurried back into town. I wondered if I would ever make the pilgrimage here again.

We later learned that Solomon and Betty were not actually buried in the earth beneath that tombstone. Their bodies had originally lain in a different Jewish cemetery. When the Nazis came to power in the 1930s, the army removed the tombstones and built bunkers; when war broke out, the Allies bombed the area. Afterward, the site was razed, the cemetery was forgotten, and a large multistoried shopping mall was constructed. The small Jewish community in Hamburg decided to erect a new memorial to Solomon in this other cemetery, remembering him for his generous contributions to Jewish life and the life of the city.

What Should We Remember?

Why have these family ties come to mean so much to me? Perhaps because none of us can know ourselves until we know something about where we have come from. Our identity is linked to our past. As I grow older, I want to learn everything I can about my Jewish heritage so that I can hand it on to my children. When I remember my Jewish ancestors, their story suddenly gives new meaning to my life; their determination, creativity, and search for a place to call home inspire me and renew my determination to surmount the challenges that I face.

But remembering is hard work, especially in a world like ours. The information era teaches us to forget yesterday's news, so that we can cram in today's. Ours is not a culture in which people sit around the campfire at night and tell stories of the ancestors; rather, we drown ourselves in mindless media diversions that enthrall us for the moment but are as memorable as potato chips are nutritious.

No wonder that we long for free zones, times and places in which we can step back and remember who we are—the family vacation that takes us back to the old homestead, the holiday celebration that gathers family members or old friends, or the quiet walk alone along a beach, down a mountain path, or through the overgrown cemetery in which our ancestors lie somewhere buried. In places like these, memories suddenly rush over us, we are overwhelmed with emotion, and we are utterly grateful again for the time that God has given us on this earth, whatever opportunities or disappointments have been our own.

Remembering takes time and space, and remembering takes practice. We have to search hard for those free zones in which we can remember again that we are really children of God. No, remembering won't come easily or automatically. On the contrary, we will fill our days with other thoughts and lose ourselves in other tasks unless remembering becomes a discipline, a way of life, for us. This kind of remembering is what the Sabbath is all about. Remember the Sabbath day so that you can remember the Lord and therefore where you have come from and who you really are.

Like the other commandments, Sabbath keeping has at times suffered from a spirit of excessive legalism or moralism. To keep Sabbath became equated with certain "dos" and "don'ts." As a child, I had older relatives who had come out of a strict Scottish Covenanter background and referred to Sunday as "the Sabbath." For them, Sabbath keeping meant going to church and refraining from worldly activities and entertainments. They understood people like Eric Liddell, the great Scottish sprinter, who went to the 1924 Olympics but was disqualified from several races because he refused to run in the preliminary heats, which fell on Sunday.

A friend of mine, of the same generation as my Covenanter relatives, has similar Sabbath memories of his childhood in the rural South. His father, a Presbyterian elder, wouldn't let his children read the Sunday comics on Sunday. They had to wait until Monday. Blue laws kept many stores and businesses closed in much of the United States, not only in the South. The concern to keep Sabbath was a Protestant phenomenon—and of special concern to Presbyterians, Methodists, and Baptists. It never had the same significance among immigrant Catholics, who regarded Sunday as a day of ethnic and religious celebration, not Sabbatarian rest. But because Protestants long dominated American culture, Sabbath keeping became culturally established. Only in my lifetime, the last fifty years or so, have rhythms of Sabbath keeping been mostly driven out of the public and into the private sphere.

Sunday is still different from the rest of the week, but no longer because of the fourth commandment. Sunday is just part of the weekend and so a day that many people have free from work. It is an extension of Saturday. Printed calendars increasingly put Saturday and Sunday together at the end of the week, with Monday, the first workday, at its beginning. Many people still go to church on Sunday (or even Saturday evening), but many more people (including many who attend church!) use Sunday to run errands that they can't get to during the workweek. Stores are open, and both professional and school-related sporting events take place. Sunday, as much as any other day, has become a time to take care of our business—a time to remember our own agenda and to get done what we need to get done.

Several years ago, my family and I drove to a crowded suburban shopping mall on a Sunday afternoon. Cars poured into the massive parking lot; customers crowded into stores, restaurants, and movie theatres. One lonely man stood by the parking lot entrance and held aloft a large sign that read, "Keep the Sabbath holy." I wondered to myself whether this man found any irony in picketing on the Lord's Day. Wasn't he working? Just what did or did not appear on his Sabbath checklist, and how did he decide? For that matter, how would any of us decide?

When Sabbath is nothing more than items on a "to do" or "not to do" list, one activity or another can easily be struck from the list and replaced by new activities that seem more compelling or interesting. But what if we see Sabbath keeping not as a list of recommended and discouraged activities but, rather, as a practice or discipline of faith, an opportunity to give specific expression to the love that we owe God? Then we cannot reduce the commandment to a mere list; it becomes, instead, an invitation to know God. The commandment offers to guide us into practices and disciplines of remembering the Holy One and our lives with him, and this remembering assures us again of our unity and identification with Jesus Christ.

In a "24 hour/7 days a week" world, Sabbath keeping is making something of a comeback. Jews and Christians are again talking about the need to set time and space aside for God. Numerous books and articles on the subject have appeared in recent years.[1] While I don't know of anyone who calls for reinstating blue laws, I have heard many individual Christians asking how they should observe Sunday specifically as the Lord's Day. Some churches have even questioned whether board and committee meetings should take place on Sunday: Must not the church itself model a different rhythm to this day? Shouldn't Sabbath matter?

But this renewed interest in Sabbath keeping is not without its ironies and contradictions. My own denomination, the Presbyterian Church (U.S.A.), recently formed a "work group" on Sabbath keeping. I have heard ministers speak of their need to keep Sabbath but then explain (or complain!) that Sunday is the last day on which they can do so. The rediscovery of Sabbath keeping sometimes seems little more than a protest against the physical and mental exhaustion that plagues too many Americans. We've been working too hard, we're tired, and we want our rest. We want time just to let go—to enjoy life again.

But Sabbath keeping is not primarily about human rest and relaxation, as legitimate as these needs are. God commands his people to keep Sabbath so that they will remember God. To keep Sabbath is to acknowledge that one day out of the week belongs not to humans and their needs, but to the Lord, our Creator, Redeemer, and Sustainer. One day out of the week, God's people should set aside their nagging concerns about everyday life and should focus, instead, on who God is and therefore who we are before God. Sabbath tells us that we cannot find our true rest through our own efforts but only as we give ourselves to the One who is our true rest.

The Comprehensive Implications of the Commandment

These deeper meanings of Sabbath come into focus if we broaden, internalize, and reverse the commandment, just as medieval and Reformation thinkers did. The commandment then: (1) becomes a broad category, (2) applies to both internal motivations and external actions, and (3) implies both a positive and a negative. Let us begin with this third aspect. As I noted in chapter 2, the Sabbath commandment explicitly reverses itself; the biblical text states both sides of the commandment. Positively, we should remember the Sabbath day and keep it holy (Exod. 20:8–9); negatively, we should not work on this day (20:10). Commentators have frequently pointed out that the Hebrew word for *rest* has the sense of "cease and desist."[2] To keep Sabbath is to drop our work, even if we have not yet completed it. If work continues to tempt us, we must turn away and say, "Get behind me, Satan!"

The second traditional move for interpreting the commandments applies them to our internal motivations. We then remember that God is concerned not only with our outer activity on the Sabbath but also with how we are disposed inwardly. Are we really remembering God? Are we honoring God in thought as well as deed? Sabbath keeping asks us to bring God back into focus in all that we do. Correspondingly, we must set aside other concerns and worries. Some early Jews insisted that one should not even think about work on the Sabbath.[3] Centuries later, the Puritan-inspired Westminster Larger Catechism similarly warned against "needless . . . thoughts about our worldly employments and recreations" (q. 119).

The first traditional interpretive move for the commandments teaches us to regard Sabbath as a broad category of motivations and actions, for work must be understood as more than paid employment or a set of daily responsibilities. Jews in particular have a long tradition of debating what exactly constitutes work. They have turned to biblical injunctions about Sabbath rest, such as: Don't bake or boil (Exod. 16:23), don't make a fire (35:3), and don't gather sticks (Num. 15:32–36). Over the centuries, authoritative rabbis added and elaborated rules, until they defined thirty-nine classes of prohibited work, and a person, for example, could not make knots on the Sabbath or walk more than two thousand cubits ("a sabbath's day journey"—see Acts 1:12) or carry an object from one place to another, except in trivial amounts.[4]

Although Christians have sometimes dismissed such prohibitions as excessively legalistic, they have faced similar challenges of defining what constitutes proper observance of the Sabbath. At least from the time of Augustine in the fifth century onward, Christian theologians have given the commandment a spiritual significance—what is required of us is not a list of "dos" or "don'ts," but nothing less than our very selves. Sabbath is not about observing one day of the week in a special way, but about submitting wholly to God. To keep Sabbath is to rest in God alone. As Scripture warns, "While the promise of entering [God's] rest is still open, let us take care that none of you should seem to have failed to reach it. . . . For we who have believed enter that rest" (Heb. 4:1, 3). God claims every part of us; everything about a Sabbath people should now flow from its identity in Christ.

If the Sabbath commandment were nothing more than a checklist of "dos" and "don'ts," we could more or less obey it. But if it asks us to give ourselves wholly to God, we will have to admit that we consistently fail. The commandment asks more of us than we can do. Nevertheless, Sabbath is more than an elusive, impossible ideal, for it has been fulfilled in Jesus Christ. The One who in love submitted himself fully to the Father and to others is the One who now offers us Sabbath rest. We do not have to create Sabbath identity by our own efforts; rather, our baptism confirms that it is already ours in Christ. Rather than condemning us for falling short, the Sabbath commandment assures us that we really belong to God and rest in him because of Christ's redemptive work. The grain of the universe runs right through us; let's go with it, not against it!

Perhaps the rabbis as they reflected on work and rest were not so different in spirit from Christians with their concern for total submission to God. To be sure, the rabbis would not have understood Sabbath keeping as growth into the image of Christ. But like Christians they would have said that covenant relationship with God frees us for a lifetime of practice and discipline. We will express our covenant identity in relation to every question that life poses. We will slowly but surely deepen our sense of God-given identity. In the Sabbath commandment, God calls us to examine every area of our lives and to conform more fully to his will. My Scottish Covenanter relatives surely understood their Sabbath regulations in a similar way—not as empty legalisms but as honoring God's claim on their lives.

We keep Sabbath, then, whenever we commemorate the fact that we are no longer our own but belong to Christ, the living Lord. We will want, of course, to live in this confidence not just on Sundays. None of our time should finally fall outside God's Sabbath time, and nothing that we do should finally escape God's claim on us. But because remembering takes practice, we nevertheless need to set aside special times and places for Sabbath keeping. Just as an athlete has a training schedule that helps him or her acquire strength more generally, so too we will schedule regular exercise time for our faith so that we can live more faithfully all the time.

This memory training does not have to be limited to Sunday. If we lived in a culture in which most of us had to work on Sunday, if the weekend fell on Tuesday and Wednesday, Christians might change their holy day. Because part of keeping Sabbath and remembering who we are is worshiping God together, we need a time when most of us can gather for worship, whether it be Sunday or Wednesday, Tuesday or Thursday.

But Sunday is an especially appropriate day for Christians to set aside, because it is the day of resurrection. The Jewish Sabbath, running from sundown on Friday to sundown on Saturday, commemorates the seventh day, the last day of the week and the day on which God rested from his creation. The Christian Sabbath begins at sunrise on the day after the seventh day of creation. On this "eighth day," as early Christians called it, God did a new thing—a thing that surpassed the creation of old. The God who neither slumbers nor sleeps quit resting, raised Jesus from the dead, and thereby restored and redeemed his people. On the eighth day, God began a new creation, a new heaven and a new earth.

We practice resting in God by remembering that God has recreated us. We are a resurrection people who participate even now in the new life in Jesus Christ. God's rest and God's work no longer stand over and against each other; they are no longer opposites. Rather, God rests most fully in himself insofar as he gives himself for the world, actively loving and redeeming it. Correspondingly, the world now rests most fully in God when it gives itself to God, glorifying and enjoying him. Sabbath keeping is about renouncing one kind of work for another—about putting aside our selfish works in order to align ourselves with God's gracious purposes.

This idea that Sabbath is as much about God's activity as about his rest appears in the biblical explanations for Sabbath keeping. Exodus appeals to the creation story and emphasizes *rest*: "For in six days the LORD made heaven and earth, the sea, and all that is in them, but rested the seventh day; therefore the LORD blessed the sabbath day and consecrated it" (Exod. 20:11). But Deuteronomy's listing of the Ten Commandments refers, instead, to the Exodus story and God's liberating *activity*: "Remember that you were a slave in the land of Egypt, and the LORD your God brought you out from there with a mighty hand and an outstretched arm; therefore the LORD your God commanded you to keep the sabbath day" (Deut. 5:15).

Sabbath commemorates a God who liberates and frees his people from their enemies and finally from their own sinfulness. To rest in God is therefore to acknowledge that we belong to him. We keep Sabbath whenever we give ourselves to the things of God—and so whenever we worship God and serve others. Jesus embodied this kind of Sabbath keeping:

> They watched him to see whether he would cure . . . on the sabbath, so that they might accuse him. . . . Then he said to them, "Is it lawful to do good or to do harm on the sabbath, to save life or to kill?" But they were silent. He looked around at them with anger; he was grieved at their hardness of heart and said to the man, "Stretch out your hand." He stretched it out, and his hand was restored." (Mark 3:2–5)

Practices and Disciplines of Sabbath Keeping

Practices and disciplines of faith help us grow in our capacity to give ourselves to God. The specific practices and disciplines of Sabbath keeping fall into three categories: (1) practices and disciplines of self-giving through *worshiping* God; (2) practices and disciplines of self-giving through *serving* others; and (3) practices and disciplines of *renouncing* the self. Together they mark us as God's own and teach us how to love God with all our heart, soul, and mind. They invite us to become more fully "a living sacrifice, holy and acceptable to God" (Rom. 12:1).

Practices and Disciplines of Self-Giving: Worship

We can say to ourselves that our true identity is in the triune God yet be plagued by doubts and diversions, for we are forgetful, neglectful creatures. We need to hear again and again who God is and who we are. As Christians over the centuries have reflected on Sabbath keeping, they have identified worship as one of its key practices, for the Word that we hear and the Supper that we share on the Lord's Day strengthen us in our baptismal identity. Word and sacrament focus us on God's promises in Scripture. Worship sends us, then, to the Bible, and not primarily for historical information or moral checklists but for the assurance that "in life and in death we belong to God."[5] The Scriptures help discipline our Sabbath memory.

As Bonhoeffer knew, practices and disciplines of Scripture reading need to shape every day, not just the Lord's Day; our life alone, as well as our life together. But even when we read the Scriptures on our own, we join implicitly with the larger community of faith. What we hear in the Scriptures—their words for each of us personally—is always framed by what we have already learned from the larger community of faith: the Sunday school classes that we attended as children, the sermons that we have heard from ministers, the books that we have read by great Christian thinkers, and the conversations that we have had with brothers and sisters in the faith.

Because we never receive God's Word as lonely, isolated selves but only as members of a covenant community, gathering for the community's worship on the Lord's Day is an especially important practice and discipline. We need to hear the Scriptures *together*, because they remind us that our baptismal identity is an identity that we share with each other. In the community's worship, Scriptures are read, preached, prayed, sung, and sacramentally enacted by and for a people. Together we drench ourselves in them and soak them up. They become our first language, our common tongue.

Nevertheless, we never read the Bible for its own sake. The words on the page matter only to the degree that they point us to God's living Word, Jesus Christ, the risen, living Lord. We depend on the Holy Spirit to illuminate these Scriptures, to guide us into them, so that we will receive them as the Word that says, "Come, follow me." To open ourselves to the Scriptures is to step into a strange, new world, where day by day we learn what it means to be a follower of Jesus. Worship draws us into Scripture, and Scripture trains us in worshiping the One who is the source of all we are and the goal of all we do.

This kind of Word-shaped worship, both personal and corporate, exercises us in self-giving love. The One who Scripture tells us has offered himself entirely to us evokes our gratitude, and we give of ourselves as we give thanks. Indeed, this gratitude *is* our self-giving. For we have nothing that we can return to God for all his goodness to us except our words of thanksgiving. To lift up our voices in adoring gratitude is to offer ourselves to God, for in thankful worship we give God our attention and place our trust in him alone. The great American Puritan theologian Jonathan Edwards employs a striking metaphor to make this point. Edwards compares God to an emanation of light. Whatever good exists in the world is but "the excellent brightness and fullness of the divinity *diffused*, *overflowing*, and as it were *enlarged*. . . . The refulgence shines upon and into the creature, and is reflected back to the luminary."[6] Humans are called to be mirrors that reflect God's glory back to him. Like a mirror, we are nothing in ourselves. We can do nothing but bear witness to God's mercy and grace—and yet in doing that, we are doing what God created us to do.

In the famous opening lines of the Westminster Shorter Catechism, "Man's chief end is to glorify God, and to enjoy him forever" (q. 1). Humans have been created to worship God by giving thanks to God for all they are and do. When Christians gather for worship, they reflect God's light both back to God and out into the world. When Christians practice Sabbath rest, they do so not only for themselves but also on behalf of the world, even when it is unbelieving. We tell the world that only when humans worship the living God do they find their deepest self.

The three commandments that precede the Sabbath commandment further specify Sabbath disciplines of self-giving gratitude:

1. "Have no other gods before me." If we are to give ourselves wholly to God, we cannot pursue other gods. We cannot let other sources of value take the place of the God of Israel and the church. No other loyalty—family, employer, nation, political party, or style of life—can be allowed to divert us from giving thanks to God for the gift of life and the gift of new life in Jesus Christ. We can give thanks for other identities, but only in and through Christ. We will need lots of practice if we are to live like the birds of the air and the lilies of the field, glorifying God by our existence and setting aside the worries of this life (see Matt. 6:25–34).

2. "Make no graven images." Many Christian traditions have regarded this commandment as part of the first; images are dangerous because they represent other gods. But Calvin and the Reformed tradition made "no graven images" a separate and second commandment, for to them, the danger was not simply other gods but the human effort to remake even the God of Israel and the church in our own image. People want a God that they can see and control. But the true God escapes our clutches. He has given himself to us in Jesus Christ, and this Jesus no longer dwells

among us but has been raised from the dead and has ascended, in the words of the Apostles' Creed, to "the right hand of God the Father Almighty." We cannot hold on to him. He has gone ahead of us.[7]

God does not promise that we will see the risen Jesus but, rather, that we will hear his Word to us. The first disciples saw him for a few days, but "blessed are those who have not seen and yet have come to believe" (John 20:29). Calvin and the Reformed tradition again wanted to point Christians to the Scriptures, not to various visual aids that threatened to take their place. The Bible is the memory bank that keeps us rightly oriented. We need again and again to hear God's words: "I have called you by name, you are mine" (Isa. 43:1). We show our gratitude to God and worship him rightly, as we open ourselves to his living Word in Scripture.

In retrospect, Calvin's judgments about images were not entirely correct. First, he failed to see that the visual arts can point us to the transcendent God without reducing God to an object of this world that we manipulate for our own purposes. Second, he failed to understand that visual images are no more subject to selfish, sinful distortion than are words, including the words of Scripture. But Calvin's larger point remains valid. We must resist not only the temptation to turn to other gods but also the temptation to distort the character of the true God. We can give ourselves to God only if we allow God to be God. True gratitude flows only from what God has done for us in Christ, not from our efforts to co-opt God for our own agenda. We will again need lots of practice if we are to approach God on his terms and not our own.

3. "Do not take the name of the Lord your God in vain." Popular piety has reduced this commandment to a question of curse words. But in its most comprehensive form, this commandment is really telling us something about the gratitude that we owe God. We cannot worship God rightly until we learn to speak rightly of God. Violations of the third commandment occur as often in churchly proclamation as in our moments of enraged, secular cursing. The Lord's name is taken in vain as often from the pulpit as in drunken brawls outside corner bars. Any of our words to and about God are frail and weak. Whatever we say about God needs God's correction.

God allows us to participate in this corrective work. He calls us to discipline our tongues. This disciplining of the words that we use to speak to God and about God is nothing less than the enterprise called theology. To think theologically is to speak as responsibly as we can about God and God's purposes. We commit ourselves to reflecting on the Scriptures and their meaning for us today. We look into every life situation and ask where and how God is at work.

Sadly, however, much of the time Christians would rather use holy words and holy things to advance themselves and their own agenda than to honor God. Mainline Protestants today fight about matters of inclusive language and whether God can ever rightly be called "he" or "Father." But issues of inclusive language matter little unless they guide us into deeper reflection on what we mean by the word *God*. Nearly all of us are tempted to speak too quickly about who God is and what righteous human cause God is advancing. Nearly all of us use the word *God* too casually, as though we could easily align him (her? Godself?) with one side of the church or another. Not taking the Lord's name in vain requires that we commit ourselves to practices and disciplines that train us in speaking gratefully and graciously about the God of grace.[8]

Thankful worship does not come without practice and discipline. To be sure, we have moments in which we pray spontaneously and intensely. We catch glimpses of God's kingdom in our corporate worship. For me, such moments sometimes come on Easter morning, when I join my voice with others' to sing the glorious hymn, "Jesus Christ Is Risen Today." In that moment, it seems to me that we are no longer separate beings with different and competing identities, but are transformed into a unified body in which each member gives himself or herself over to the One who holds everything together. We stand in the presence of One greater than ourselves. He has given us a common name: We are children of the Father, Son, and Holy Spirit. But once we have caught such glimpses, we know that we cannot live from them alone. The word *liturgy* means "the work of the people," and worship will take work—careful planning and execution, and not only on the part of the worship leaders. Worship is a team sport in which all of us are involved. Each of us must practice giving our attention to God. The thanks that we owe God is not so much a passing emotional high as a self-giving way of life that begins and ends in worshiping him.

Worship reminds us that God created us for himself so that we might know the divine glory and increase that glory by glorifying God. Worship offers us a free zone in which we can risk being the people that God has created us to be. Worship teaches us that we should have no other gods; that God comes to us on his terms, not our own; and that we are created to speak rightly of God and his purposes for us. To be a child of the God who is Father, Son, and Holy Spirit is to grow in the ability to say "thank you" for each new day, whatever challenges and opportunities it brings.

Even thanksgiving can become distorted, however, and gratitude can become nothing other than an expression of pride and selfishness: "God, I thank you that I am not like other people: thieves, rogues, adulterers, or even like this tax collector" (Luke 18:11). But worship that draws us into God's living Word bases gratitude not in the identities that we would give ourselves, but in the identity that Christ has won for us by giving himself up to death, even death on a cross.

Practices and Disciplines of Self-Giving: Service

One of the great insights of the Christian tradition is that worship leads to service, gratitude to good works. The giving of ourselves that God makes possible turns us not only to him but also to others. The first table of the law underlies and advances the second: "We love because he first loved us. . . . The commandment we have from him is this: those who love God must love their brothers and sisters also" (1 John 4:19, 21). Worship and ethics are not opposites. Glorifying God and reaching out to one another in love do not contradict each other. On the contrary, neither is possible without the other. They are part of the same fabric of self-giving love that is now our true identity in Jesus Christ.

Ethics is not first of all about the things that we do, but about the life that we are asked to offer each other. This lesson struck me again last April. Spring had finally come to Pittsburgh after a long, cold winter. Never had we seen such intense spring colors. In other years, a hot spell followed by hard rains had quickly knocked blossoms off the trees, but this year they lasted for weeks. One Sunday afternoon was finally warm enough for me to announce to the family, "Today we are going to have Kaffee Trinken."

Over the years, we have made many friends in Germany, and when Germans have guests on a Sunday afternoon, you can be sure that they will brew a pot of coffee and offer them cake or chocolates. As we sat in our American backyard, far from our German friends, we remembered the many times that we have been privileged to sit in one of their beautiful gardens, sipping a cup of coffee and enjoying each other's company.

A foreigner often fells vulnerable and needy. You never quite fit. The language is strange, the customs are unfamiliar, and you don't always know how to negotiate even the simpler matters of life. Just walking into a grocery store can be a frightening experience! So to have a safe place to sit and drink coffee can be deeply moving—you suddenly know that there are people who are willing to make space for you. What is remarkable about such experiences is finally not the coffee or the conversation, but the fact that people have given something of themselves to you. They have taken time and made efforts on your behalf.

Such moments of self-giving become Sabbath free zones just as worship is. We sit in the warm sunshine and take in the beauty of the moment, knowing that this moment will never come again in precisely this way. We are thankful. Indeed, a foreigner has little more to return to his or her hosts than these meager words of thanks! But thanksgiving is not only a matter of a word or two; rather, it is to be set into a way of life in which you practice giving yourself to others, as limited and inadequate as your efforts seem.

Christian ethics is thus the art of giving of ourselves in love and gratitude to others, especially to those who are as vulnerable as the foreigner that each of us has been at one time or another. Just as the first three commandments explicate the way of giving ourselves to God, the six commandments that follow the Sabbath commandment explicate the way of giving ourselves to others. I will pursue this point in greater detail in chapters 4 and 5. Suffice it now to say that the Sabbath commandment calls us to give witness to God's liberating work by liberating others from our normal, everyday demands on them. One day a week, at least on the Lord's Day, we should practice giving each other space.

Everyday life involves constantly negotiating the differing interests, needs, and priorities of diverse individuals. Inevitably, each of us wants the world to revolve around ourselves. But we quickly come up against others who are equally sure that the world, we included, should revolve around them. Democracy has taught Americans the value of balancing these competing interests, finding workable compromises, and debating and weighing the merits of each position. But democracy does not eliminate self-interest. To paraphrase Winston Churchill, "Democracy is a bad form of government, but the alternatives are even worse." Even a vibrant democracy is not yet the kingdom of God, in which "the wolf shall live with the lamb, . . . the calf and the lion and the fatling together" (Isa. 11:6). The truth is that a world of competing interests exhausts most of us by the end of the day. We grow weary of having to exercise eternal vigilance in order to protect our property, our families, our careers, and our lives.

I think of my little corner of Pittsburgh, the two miles that stretch between my house and the seminary. Most properties are meticulously kept, but I often see people drive down a busy street and throw their fast-food trash out the car window. Running red lights has become second nature. Booming car stereos shake the windows of our house, 150 feet away from the street. In the nearby park, people regularly let their dogs off-leash right by the sign that says, "Dogs must be on a leash." Despite these dirty smudges on the cityscape, the world continues to function; life pretty much goes on. But a toll is exacted. One is never quite sure who will do what next. Stress levels rise and sometimes become frustrated rage.

The world of work is no different. It may be less anonymous than city spaces; we know our colleagues and have to get along with them. But we as often disappoint as delight each other. It seems as though we cannot keep every colleague happy at the same time. In such a world, it is not surprising that we get twenty years into our work and suddenly understand how a person might want to retire someday. The pace is demanding; the endless negotiating wears us out. Family life presents similar challenges: Kids and parents have different and sometimes conflicting needs; what is good for one spouse may not be good for another.

As we have seen, worship promises us Sabbath free space. Of course, worship can become politicized as congregations debate different worship styles or the merits of a particular pastor's preaching, but worship at its heart nevertheless calls us to step back and begin practicing a different way of life together. We then remember that we have a different identity from that of the self-interested competitor. Worship's free zone should therefore encourage us in the practice and discipline of creating additional free spaces for each other. To be sure, we cannot change the world entirely, even if we can make it better; in the end, we have to hope for another reality, a divine order, before which this world will ultimately pass away. But in the midst of this conflicted world here and now, we can nevertheless be those mirrors that cast God's light into the darkness. We can create provisional, temporary free zones in which we relate to each other as children of God. Sabbath keeping is less about getting rest and relaxation for ourselves than about offering life-giving relationship to others.[9]

Where can we reach out to others? In Puritan piety, the Lord's Day was a day not only for worship but also for visiting the sick and the poor. How might we use Sabbath time to care for each other?

Where can we release others from our normal, everyday demands on them? God commanded that even slaves and animals should get rest on this day. How can we give others the space that they need to be themselves and not simply instruments to the fulfillment of our own needs?

Sabbath time is about liberating others so that they can find their identity in God. We step back from imposing an identity upon them. How might we remember that God has marked every human being as his own?

The Sabbath commandment is thus the cornerstone of the whole Decalogue.[10] It tells us that grateful worship and service constitute our true identity. It points us to God and to others. If we finally do need rest and relaxation for ourselves, it is because we need to be able to give of ourselves more fully and freely; to the degree that we are tired and harassed, we tend to turn in on ourselves, obsessed with our own problems and burdens. Sabbath time turns us outward again—but, as we have seen, we will still need lots of practice if we are truly to rest in God alone.

Practices and Disciplines of Self-Renunciation[11]

As much as we say that we long for Sabbath rest, most of us really do prefer to wallow in our weariness. Ironically, we have to work at not working. It is not easy for us to put our own agenda aside; our everyday labors may tire us out, but we also derive a great deal of our identity from them.

I know how hard it is to turn off the conversation in our heads when we come to worship. Although I am ordained, I sit in the pew most Sundays—a seminary professor, but just another member of the congregation. The pastor reads the Scriptures and begins preaching, and I am as apt as the next person to let my mind wander. I think about all the things I should be doing, the demands of work and home. I worry about whether anyone really cares about my efforts—the classes I teach, the books I write. I grow irritated when the preacher is superficial; has so little to say but takes so many words to say it. Coming to worship takes practice and discipline, also for me.

It is hard for me to put aside my everyday tasks in order to make Sabbath time for others. I resist Sabbath time. Too often, a self-pitying voice inside me declares that my hard work at the office already serves others, and that I am probably giving away too much of myself as it is—after all, I teach and encourage students, serve on faculty committees, preach in congregations, and write for the wider church. Ironically, however, this workload makes me protective, not self-giving. I hunker down in my office in front of the computer screen and come out only for scheduled events. I do not easily find time to sit with others, simply taking delight in their existence. I do not easily make free zones in which I can relate to others not only through my work agenda but also through our shared identity as brothers and sisters in Christ. Learning to be a good host, to invite people into my space, and to release them from my everyday demands on them is not all that easy. I, like others, have to work at making spaces like Kaffee Trinken on a beautiful spring Lord's Day afternoon.

We all have to work at not having other gods; at not reducing God to a plaything; at not speaking about life as though God were far away, disinterested and disengaged. As Calvin once noted, "We shall have to labor hard . . . [to renounce] all our thoughts and desires in such a way that only God governs us."[12]

But God has given us space in which to practice. God has not demanded that we achieve perfection, only that we grow into the perfection that is already ours in Jesus Christ. God has given us practices and disciplines along whose paths the Holy Spirit moves in order to strengthen us in our identity in Christ. God has given us free zones of worship and service in which we might again remember who we really are. We will have to search for these free zones as carefully as my family and I had to search for Solomon Heine's grave, but in the end they are as close as our brothers and sisters in Christ. The way of life to which God calls us is life together, and we can practice opening up free zones whenever we come together.

Sabbath Free Zones

In reflecting on Sabbath, Karl Barth clarified the nature of these free zones.[13] He suggests four ways in which we can express Sabbath freedom: Sabbath will be (1) a day without a rigid schedule, (2) a day of joy, (3) a day of fellowship, and (4) a day that flows into the rest of the week. Each of these aspects of Sabbath freedom suggests practices and disciplines that we need if the Holy Spirit is to train us in self-giving gratitude.

1. Sabbath is a day without a rigid schedule. Most of us live by the watch and the calendar. Whether we are organized people or not, life forces us to keep track of time. But Sabbath reminds us that man was not made for the schedule but the schedule for man. Barth suggests that we need one day a week, the Lord's Day, on which to let the day unfold as it will. Even the Lord's Day will have a schedule, of course. We will want to get to church on time. We will want to be able to eat and get from one place to another. But perhaps on this one day we can also afford to live a bit more spontaneously. We might run into someone at church and ask that person over for lunch or Kaffee Trinken. We might decide on the spur of the moment to play ball with our kids or pack up the family for a walk in the woods.

2. Sabbath is a day of joy. In the medieval church, the Lord's Day was always a day of feasting. If you have ever wondered why we speak of the *forty* days of Lent, even though there are *forty-six* days from Ash Wednesday to Easter Sunday, it is because the medieval church did not count the six Sundays. Lent was a season of fasting, in which the church remembered that Jesus had fasted forty days in the wilderness. But medieval Catholics never fasted on the Lord's Day, and ironically, when a person did fast on Sunday, some penitential handbooks imposed a penalty of additional days of fasting![14] (Would not the more suitable punishment have been days of feasting?) Other Christian traditions, as well as Judaism, have also emphasized the festal character of Sunday. When I was growing up, my mother always brought out the good china for Sunday dinner after church. Even before we children could hold a fork properly, we ate from her best plates. Sunday dinner was a special time. Some families today choose special foods for Sunday; my family's habit is to prepare a batch of nachos at lunch, and to have ice cream for dessert after supper.

3. Sabbath is a day of fellowship. People should feel free on this day to make special plans with others. We can gather together for joyful celebration. We can share meals and do things together as families. Some of the penitential handbooks of the Middle Ages dictated that monks wash the feet of any laymen who happened to be in the monastery on that day, for Sunday was to be a day of generous hospitality.[15] Today some of us will want to practice traditional Reformed habits of Lord's Day hospitality by visiting those in need—or we can at least phone loved ones or write a letter or send an e-mail.[16] Others of us will open our homes to friends and strangers, inviting them into our space and our lives.

4. Sabbath is a day that flows into the rest of the week. Sabbath gives us practice time, but we need not stop practicing spontaneity, joy, and fellowship when Monday arrives. Every day can include elements of spontaneity. I think of a friend of mine who kept a detailed calendar. Whenever he got his new calendar for the year, he would write the word *something* in each of the blank boxes. If someone then phoned him up and asked him to come to a meeting that he really didn't want to attend, he would say, "Just a minute. Let me look at my calendar. Oh, I'm sorry,

I already have 'something' on it." It was his little protest against an over-scheduled world, his way of scheduling, paradoxically, the spontaneous freedom of life before God.

Every day of the week can be shaped by Sabbath joy, especially the joy of worship and Christian service. We can practice daily prayer alone and with others. We can practice giving others moments of delight. Every day of the week can also include elements of fellowship. Bonhoeffer, for example, saw every mealtime as an invitation to Sabbath.[17] Too often I eat my lunch in front of my computer screen as I work away. I would benefit by the discipline of once or twice a week eating lunch with one of my students or colleagues—getting out of the office, sitting at table, and enjoying life together.

Spontaneity, joy, and fellowship characterize the self-giving gratitude that belongs to the children of God. Each aspect of Sabbath freedom has something childlike about it, for children—if they are able to live in the free zones of childhood—exhibit spontaneity, joy, and fellowship. So, too, we must again become like children, if we are to enter the kingdom of God. The paradox is that we will have to work at it, yet it is already who we really are—children of God.

The Topography of Faith

A free zone is not an imaginary time and place. It has a history and a topography, a when and where. The Jewish cemetery in Hamburg is a free zone for me; its peaceful paths and wild beauty draw me into deeper gratitude for my life. It is a place to which I can make pilgrimage. Even if I never returned, I would derive deep comfort from the fact that I had once stood there, in front of that marble tombstone in a neatly ordered corner of an otherwise overgrown cemetery. Yes, I have been there. Solomon's gravesite does exist. Were it someday to be destroyed, I would lose something precious, but not everything—because I have memories, and I have others who have accompanied me there and can help me remember.

Each of us needs free zones, times and places that link us to the past and to the wider world of which we constitute only one tiny part and, nevertheless, of which *we* are a part. Above all, we need Sabbath free zones—a history and topography of faith, times and places in which we can regularly remember our lives in relation to God, God's people, and the whole of God's creation, as minuscule as any of us are in that greater scheme of things.

The God of the fourth commandment is not a nameless abstraction but a God who has established a history and topography of his own—times and places in which people have been able to meet him, even though he is also beyond time and place and meeting. The God of Israel has intervened in human affairs by speaking words of judgment and grace. The God of the church has sent us a Son, who has lived, died, and risen to new life in our very midst. God has entered history and taken up space by becoming flesh, breath, and blood. This God continues to meet his people today as his Holy Spirit acts in Word, sacrament, and the disciplined practices of the community of faith. This God creates free zones.

The people of Israel and the church came to think of the commandments as timeless truths, but the revelation of these truths nevertheless came at a definite time and place. They reminded the people of a God who had intervened in their lives in order to make his will known and to draw his people back to their true selves.

God had delivered his people from Egypt. He had brought them safely through the wilderness. They now stood at the foot of the great mountain, Sinai (see Exod. 19). Moses went up the mountain on their behalf, and God descended upon it in smoke and lightning. But God did not aim at simply overwhelming Moses and the people. God did not reveal himself so that Moses and the people would only cower before him, as though he were too great or powerful or wonderful for them ever to get near. Rather, God spoke. God spoke words. God spoke words that people could hear and understand and carry in their hearts. God spoke words by which people could mark themselves as God's own.

The first words that God spoke reminded the people of who this God was—a God who was known not in the mystery of his transcendence but in the graciousness of his presence, a God who had chosen to create a world and enter history and to live in relationship with a people. He declared, "I am the LORD your God, who brought you out of the land of Egypt, out of the house of slavery" (Exod. 20:2). This promise, the prologue to the Ten Commandments, was so important to the people of Israel that they counted it as part of the first commandment. God's "first word" to Israel was not about what should mark their lives, but about what already characterized and always would characterize God's life: his will to deliver a people. The commandments began with a word about God, not us.

But God did not leave the people without the ability to speak a word of their own in response. The injunctions that followed God's declaration of his character to them were to be the people's declaration of theirs to him. The people were to commit themselves to the way of life that God revealed in the commandments. And Sabbath keeping was not just one item out of many on the list. Rather, Sabbath keeping was the invitation to commit themselves to the way of all the commandments.

To keep the Sabbath day holy is to remember God, the Deliverer. The fourth commandment calls us to remember the concrete, specific circumstances in which the people of Israel received all ten, and to practice entering the free zones that God has given us for loving and worshiping him and loving and serving one another in Christ's name. Sabbath invites us to lose ourselves in praise and adoration of God, and to reach out to people in need, seeing them as our brothers and sisters. Sabbath opens up time and space for us to "re-collect" the fragments of our lives and thus to practice our baptismal identity.

Chapter Four

Homecoming

> Honor your father and your mother, so that your days may be long in the land that the LORD your God is giving you.
>
> Exod. 20:12

We all have places that help us remember who we really are, such as my Jewish cemetery in Hamburg. But there are also people who help us remember who we are; in my case, a father and a mother.

I wish that I remembered more about my father. He died when I was nineteen, a sophomore in college. The summer after I graduated from high school in San Antonio, Texas, my parents moved to Atlanta, Georgia, while I went off to Colorado Springs, Colorado, to begin college. I visited them at winter break. A couple months later, my mother phoned me that my father, at age forty-seven, had sustained a mild heart attack. I was deeply shaken. But my mother seemed hopeful. There was no need for me to fly home; he was recovering well in the hospital. Those days in the hospital turned out to be a high point of my father's life. He had always lived life intensely, and now he seemed to savor each moment all the more. He later made a tape recording in which he expressed his gratitude for all who had reached out to him: the nurses, the doctors, his wife and children, and the hundreds of friends and family members who had sent cards or written notes or made telephone calls. He expressed his deep desire to live longer, especially for the sake of watching his children grow up. But he was also profoundly grateful for the years that he had been given. He had no doubt that he had already lived a rich, full life.

When summer came, I returned home briefly. My father was doing well. He had returned to work; life seemed normal. The one difference was that he had added a walk to his daily regimen, and I accompanied him several times. His doctors, though, had concerns about other blockages that might appear, and in those days, open-heart surgery was not yet routinely performed. If we started up a hill and he felt tightness in his chest, he popped a nitroglycerine pill under his tongue.

I was home again at Christmas; my father continued to do well. But three months later, on March 26, 1974, only a few days after a medical check-up and almost a year to the day of his first heart attack, he had a second. A business trip had taken him back to San Antonio. While walking down a busy city street, he had collapsed. A policeman had seen him fall and had run over to offer assistance. But there was nothing to do; he had died instantly.

My father had been my best friend. I knew practically every hair on his head—when I was a kid, he would ask me on Sunday afternoons to give him a head scratch, or to massage his tense neck muscles. I would notice his warts and blemishes, his strength and build. I had so often confided in him; we shared many interests. For a decade after his death, I struggled with depression. I had lost a part of myself that I could never retrieve. A part of my life had simply vanished. The man who had cared for me since childhood, who had connected me to a larger family past, and who had embodied many of my ideals was suddenly gone—the one person besides my mother who could best help me remember my God-given identity.

Since then, I have relied all the more on my mother to keep me connected to my past. She has become the repository of family history, the bearer and caretaker of our collective memories, including memories of my father and his side of the family. When my siblings and I have wanted to remember a detail of our childhood or have wondered again what Dad was really like, we have turned to her. In the first years after my father's death, she also relied on me in new ways. I was the oldest of her four children, and when she needed counsel about financial decisions or house repairs or family problems, she asked me to help. I was not fully prepared for that role, and in retrospect I wish that I had played it better. By age nineteen, young men in North American society are beginning to separate themselves emotionally from their mothers, and I was looking for my own identity—the one that I would create, rather than the one that I had simply by virtue of being an obedient son. My mother's new emotional dependence on me sometimes weighed me down; perhaps even more difficult was the realization that despite all my desire to be independent and self-identifying, I needed her more than ever.

Now, thirty years after my father's death, I stand in awe of the unwavering love and support that my mother has given my siblings and me over our lifetimes, even in those dark days after my father's death. She continues to hold her family together, relaying news from one child or relative to another and ensuring that we, who are scattered to the four winds, get together at least once a year. But none of us is getting younger; I am now older than my father when he died. My mother is retired, and she is slowly putting the legacy of a lifetime in order: old photos, papers, and family heirlooms. Recently, she has been rereading and sharing the letters that my father sent her during their engagement fifty years ago. I remember my parents best during their midlife years when the pressures and stresses of work and raising a family made for busy schedules and, sometimes, short tempers; the letters remind me how much they were in love with each other.

A few years ago, my mother and I decided to visit her childhood home in upstate New York. First, we drove to the rural area where my mother's grandmother and several aunts and uncles had lived. I had childhood memories of the old family farm and house, of my Aunt Rosa who had lived there, and of her brother Uncle Will who had lived nearby. My father and I had once flown a kite on the old farmstead—at the time, it seemed to fly so high as to be nearly out of sight. The old family home held even more memories for my mother—memories of her childhood, her grandmother, and family holidays. The house no longer seemed so big, nor the farm so remote, as it had appeared to me as a child. We stopped at the two cemeteries in which family members lay buried. The day was quiet and peaceful, and my mother and I took our time walking among the graves and finding the tombstones for her parents and grandparents. Then we drove to the neighborhood in Buffalo in which my mother had grown up and her parents had lived until their deaths in the early 1970s.

We had visited my grandparents every other summer when I was a boy, and I remembered the evenings when they and my parents sat chatting under the old oak tree in the backyard while my brothers and I listened from an upstairs bedroom window—we always had a hard time going to sleep at Grandma and Grandpa's, because the summer light lasted so late into the night. After my grandparents' death, my mother had sold the house. Now, more than thirty years later, we did not try to go inside. But we were pleased that the exterior had been neatly maintained and still resembled the house that we had once known. I took a photo; we slowly returned to the car and continued our memory tour. Every stop along the way offered opportunity for another photo: my mother in front of her elementary school, my mother in front of her high school, and my mother in front of the church in which she had grown up and had been married. We drove by the ice cream parlor that she had frequented as a girl, not far from the University of Buffalo, from which she had graduated. We had coffee with the woman who had been her sixth-grade teacher.

That evening, as we headed back to my home in Pittsburgh, we grew silent, alone in our own thoughts. My mother had entrusted me with these pieces of her life, and I was deeply moved. She had honored me with her memories, and I would now honor her by caring for them.

But perhaps the most important memory of all was this newest, most recent experience—the trip itself, the time that the two of us had spent together. I felt that we were no longer just mother and son, but two people bound together by a common history and aware of our common humanity and mortality. I knew that both of us saw the years flying by and that both of us wondered what it would mean someday to die. Neither of us could imagine life without the other, because our lives had become so intertwined over the years.

The Meaning of Honor

That trip with my mother made me realize how little Christians these days talk about parents and children. There is a great deal of Christian literature about parenting, and some, especially from more conservative quarters, about the obedience that children owe parents. But how often do we talk about why people should or should not have children, or what it means to watch one's parents grow older and one's relationship to them change? Mainline denominations fight about how to understand sexual relationships, but they do much less to help people think about a relationship that is as profoundly intimate and complicated: that of child to parent, and of parent to child.[1]

Part of the challenge in talking about family relations these days is our awareness of many different kinds of families. Children are not always raised by their biological parents, and some families are led by a single person or a homosexual couple. Not every parent is loving. Even those of us who had "good" parents know that family life is often messy. I nevertheless came home from my trip with my mother giving thanks for the joys and privileges of our life together. She and my father gave me life. They cared for me when I was still too weak to care for myself. They taught me my first lessons in life and helped shape my identity. They were the people who first gave me a home and who so often helped me to come back home to my true identity when I found myself lost and wandering in the wilderness of life. Over the years, my mother's love has reassured me that I was not only her child but also a child of God!

In response to whatever good our parents have done for us, we should *honor* them, although this honor will take different forms in different family situations. The fifth commandment does not tell us that we must always like our parents or agree with them. Many parents and children feel a natural affection for and loyalty to each other, but relationships between parents and children also have areas of tension. Parents sometimes feel irritation, even anger, at their children and the demands that they make. Children sometimes come to resent the limitations that parents place on them. Life in families is always evolving; it never reaches an easy equilibrium.[2] Because of the complexities of family relationships, honoring father and mother, like keeping Sabbath, is best understood not as a single act but as a set of practices and disciplines at which we will work over a lifetime. The honor that we owe parents has to be more than a spontaneous feeling of affection, more than a mere confirmation of common interests. Like people in other kinds of vital relationships, parents and children will spend their entire lives learning how (and even whether) to live with each other.

My trip with my mother nevertheless taught me why honor was indeed the right thing for me to show her. In light of what we had shared, I felt called to let my mother's life weigh upon me and be weighty to me.[3] I wanted to value her history and identity as part of my own history and identity, and to respect the legacy of her life, care for it, treasure it, and take delight in it. Something more significant than even tenderness or agreeability had touched us; I had experienced profound humility and awe as I contemplated the fact of my mother's life. My mother and I have sometimes gotten on each other's nerves; we have sometimes disagreed. Our relationship has not been perfect. But our lives are inseparable, and the history that we share calls out to be honored.

Honor as Submission

We should honor our parents, because our life is finally rooted in theirs. None of us can "do life" just on our own. We cannot make a home in this world by ourselves. None of us has brought himself or herself into existence, and none of us is purely self-made. We have a history that began with our biological parents and was shaped by them and/or others who raised us. To the degree that we maintain a relationship with these individuals, we honor them whenever we acknowledge that we have depended on them. In this sense, honor includes an element of submission.

Contemporary Americans do not like the word *submission*. Submission implies a hierarchy, one who commands and one who obeys. We fear that submission leads to oppression, that those with power will inevitably misuse it and those without power will be exploited. As members of a democratic society, we assume that the best guarantor of right relationship is a sharing of power. Vital, healthy relationships will be egalitarian. People will regard each other as equals. We prefer to think of relationships in terms of partnership rather than of submission, of mutual affirmation rather than of humility.

But to honor another is to acknowledge that he or she has a claim on us, a claim to which we must submit. Submission is not the only thing that we owe the other, but life together is not possible without it. We let the other weigh down upon us, so that we can be in relationship with the other. Again, this kind of honoring and submitting does not come naturally or easily. It will take practice and discipline, and we must learn what kind of submitting strengthens a relationship and what kind distorts it.

Learning submission does not mean simply reading and obeying a list of "dos" and "don'ts." Rather, families from their beginnings have to develop *patterns*—that is, practices and disciplines—of submission that will become richer and more complex over time. A child has to learn not only to submit to others but also to command their submission to him or her. Moreover, a child has to learn how to weave submission into a larger tapestry of attitudes and dispositions that make family life possible, such as trust, respect, cooperation, and care.

Our first experience of submission is as a baby, utterly dependent on our mother for food and protection. A baby cannot have life on its own terms; at the same time, it is not a passive, inert object. It makes demands; it asks to be honored. As it cries out in the middle of the night and its tiny lungs gasp for air, it declares, "Well, here I am. What are you going to do about it?" A good parent knows that a baby is meant for freedom as well as submission, for independence as well as dependence—and in the years ahead, a good parent will give a baby opportunity to grow in both directions.

The baby grows into a little boy. The parents lay down rules and set boundaries that they expect him to respect. They order his life and ask him to conform to what they believe to be right and good for him. They determine when he wakes up, what he wears, and how he spends his time. They determine his contact with the larger world—whether he ever goes to church or not, or watches a particular television program, or plays with the neighbor's children. But, again, the parents' determinations are never absolute. Part of growing up is discovering one's expanding opportunities to assert oneself and to make claims on others, even to manipulate them, as young children seem to discover all too quickly. A good parent knows how to give children enough space to make decisions for themselves, and how to let them learn from the consequences of their actions.

As the little boy becomes a young man, his parents impose fewer conditions on his life; parents and child increasingly have to reach decisions together. Just as in a business corporation or another social organization, negotiation and compromise become essential, and persuasion becomes more important than force. Submission is no longer a given. Rather, it is something that the child can choose or reject.

Yet submission will always play a role in the child's life. He will learn that always getting his way at the expense of others can carry a huge price. His parents still have resources that he needs—not only power and money but, even more importantly, wisdom, life experience, and emotional support. Family life teaches the joys and frustrations of interdependence, and even though the shape and parameters of that interdependence change, it never disappears, so long as parent and child are in living relationship with each other.

The child becomes a man who marries and begins a family of his own. The parents now have not only a son but also a daughter-in-law and grandchildren. Once again, parents and child have to renegotiate the fabric of interdependence. That fabric may become thicker or thinner, richer in patterns or poorer. Parents and child can never know in advance about the life events that will bring unexpected twists and turns, knots and rips, to their relationship. But a child, even a grown child, discovers that he cannot maintain a relationship to his parents without submitting at one point or another to them. He will not always submit when and where he would choose. If a parent suddenly says, "I need you," or "Please, help me," the child knows that honoring the relationship and acknowledging its weight in his life requires his presence and attention.

Years fly by, and one day the parent finds that he or she increasingly submits to the child. The father has Parkinson's, or the mother is suddenly widowed. Money is tight; the parents can no longer keep up the house. In the meantime, the son has his own life to live; he has his own family that demands his time. But his father and mother are becoming older and more vulnerable, and they too demand more of his attention. The son may have much or little to do with them on a daily basis, but someday he may have to make key decisions about their living and dying, more so than he ever could have imagined or wished.

Yet even here the parents never become inanimate, impersonal objects. Even if the father or the mother someday lies unconscious on a hospital bed, he or she will still make a claim on the son. The son will not be able to look at his parents without remembering a living relationship. The fabric of interdependence will be rewoven but not discarded, as the child tries to understand what honor means, even in such difficult circumstances as these.

A consumer society underplays the importance of interdependence, teaching us instead that we deserve to have things *our* way. The egalitarian, democratic features of our society further encourage us to think about our personal, individual worth, and about our "right" to be affirmed by others and to determine ourselves. And here is the tension, for family life teaches us that dependence is as basic a reality as independence; self-denial is as essential as self-fulfillment. If we are ever going to find our way home, if we are ever going to know who we really are, letting others get their way at our expense will sometimes be as important as getting our way at their expense. We will have to learn when and how to practice submission, for the sake of learning to live in relationship with others.

In sum, the fifth commandment captures an essential, universal truth: God has created humans for life in families, and life in families requires us to learn practices and disciplines of submission. This kind of submission is neither self-deprecating nor self-destructive, but is rather a matter of letting others weigh down upon us. The parent must sometimes submit to the child, the child sometimes to the parent. But rarely if ever will they confront each other merely as self-sufficient equals, even in a society that speaks so eloquently of equality.

This training in submission also trains one in humility. A central insight of the Christian tradition has been that sin expresses itself primarily as pride. Every person would like to make himself or herself the center of the universe. We want the world to serve our purposes and to fulfill our needs. But family life teaches us that ours is not the only place. We stand next to others who also have their rightful place. In families, we learn to see how we fit with others into a larger scheme of things.

At the same time, this training in submission and humility does not simply "put us in our place" but also gives us a place that is really and uniquely our own. The Christian tradition has noted that sloth is every bit as dangerous as pride. When afflicted by sloth, we doubt that we have a place in the universe. We acquiesce to inner voices of doubt and despair.

We refuse to believe that our lives are meaningful and good. Family life calls us back into the land of living. It assures us that our place in this universe, however small, is precious and honorable.

As an adolescent, the child may be embarrassed that his parents are nothing more than this man and this woman, with all their warts and blemishes. The parents' wisdom and goodness suddenly seem so limited and insignificant in comparison with the powers that the adolescent is discovering for himself in the wider world. But it is precisely this man and this woman who look at their son and tell him that he is irreplaceable. He can never escape their shadow, yet it is in this shadow that he can see how much his life matters. He is of infinite value to persons who are so embarrassingly finite, and that inescapable fact will always prove humbling yet immensely comforting to him.

In describing the moral order that God has established and in which God invites us to participate, the fifth commandment also has key social import, for the family's training in submission, humility, and interdependence prepares children for life with others outside the family. Our parents (and our siblings, if we have any) are the first neighbors that we encounter, and what we learn growing up in a family shapes the way we relate to others in the larger world. Social life, even in an egalitarian world, can never be based on a principle of self-assertion alone. Family life prepares us to negotiate the claims that humans make on each other in the wider world—claims that flow as often out of inequality as equality, out of our vulnerability as much as our power, and out of our weakness as much as our strength.

Human societies have generally concluded that parents and families shape children for responsible citizenship far more effectively than other social structures can, including the state. The state should therefore support and strengthen family life, so that children will grow up learning to respect others and care for them. When families fall apart, social stability is ultimately threatened.[4]

How Families Can Practice the Faith

Yet families have the power to distort our being as well as to nourish it; to teach us distrust as well as trust. They can help us to thrive, or they can make us think of ourselves as helpless victims or as angry victimizers. They influence for good or ill our view of God and whether we come to regard the ultimate powers of life as benevolent or malicious; gracious, or judgmental and condemning.

What finally enables families to develop patterns of interdependence, such that we learn to give honor to others where it is due them and to command honor from others where it is due us? How does family life stay grounded in the fifth commandment? Patterns of submission, humility, and interdependence will inevitably become distorted and destructive unless they finally invite each member of the family into deeper relationship with God.

Christian parents are ultimately concerned that their children learn to live not only with others but also—and primarily—before God. The Christian tradition has argued that children first come to know God as they relate to their parents. Our childhood dependence on our parents teaches us that we are by nature dependent creatures, whose lives are ultimately sustained by God alone. Similarly, the goodness and wisdom that we find in our parents teaches us about the One who is the source of all goodness and wisdom.

Yet family life does not automatically lead its members into right knowledge of God. Christian parents recognize how far they fall short of adequately representing God to their children. Submission to parents must become submission to God if children are to learn the kind of submission to parents that truly pleases God. The greatest gift that a parent can give a child is not a capacity for blind obedience, but a sense of his or her baptismal identity—that is, the certainty that in life and in death, he or she belongs to God, not to father or mother.

Parents sustain a child in her baptismal identity as they take the dramatic and terrifying step of delivering their baby out of their own hands into the hands of God. They let the child pass through the waters of baptism; they allow her to receive her true, Trinitarian name; and they take a vow "to live the Christian faith, and to teach that faith to [their] child." As they stand at the front of the sanctuary, they hear a congregation promise to "guide and nurture [this child], by word and deed, with love and prayer, encouraging [her] to know and follow Christ, and to be a faithful member of his church."[5] The Christian tradition (and especially Reformed theology) has often pointed out that baptism is as much for the parents and the community of faith as for the child. Baptism not only confirms a child's identity in Christ but also issues a call to each of us. It asks us to take a pledge to sustain our own baptismal identity, as well as the child's.

Baptism sets an entire family on a journey. The baby comes out of the waters, and the minister hands her back to the parents; now they must reshape family life in a way that will remind their child again and again who she really is. The practices and disciplines that Bonhoeffer described for his community at Finkenwalde are suggestive of what might happen in a different but no less powerful way in families: a deepening of identity in Word, sacrament, and life together.

A family can develop practices and disciplines of the Word. The Puritans spoke of the family as a little church; family devotions played a key role. One or more times a day, the family gathered to practice the four elements of daily prayer that Bonhoeffer described: psalms, Scriptures, singing, and praying. Reformation theologians such as Luther entrusted parents with teaching their children the catechism, with its explication of the church's basic theology (Apostles' Creed), ethics (the Decalogue), and worship practices (the Lord's Prayer and the sacraments).[6] The Reformers believed that parents also had the responsibility to see that their children participated in the life of the church. The commandment to keep Sabbath was understood to lay on father and mother the duty to bring their children to Lord's Day worship.[7] Parents might play a key role in educating their children in the faith, but they could not play the only role. They needed the wisdom of the wider community of faith. Affirming their child's baptismal identity meant that they gave their child a home in the church.

Today, even while some parents are beginning to rediscover the critical role of the family in training children in faith, many others do not fully grasp the significance of their role and how much more important it has become in a pluralistic world. Christians cannot and should not expect public schools to help with the transmission of Christian identity. They cannot and should not rely on cultural props that the church once enjoyed, such as state-enforced Sabbath keeping or state-sponsored prayer at civic events. They must assume new responsibility for helping their children practice their baptismal identity.

Many parents, feeling that they do not have the ability to form their children in the faith, turn to the church, asking it to offer Sunday school programs and youth group activities. Yet competing activities, such as school sporting events, often get in the way. Every pastor these days knows of parents who are solid members of the church yet insist that their children must give priority to other activities. Families too often decide that it is more important to discipline their children in social values of success and achievement than in Christian faith. Family rhythms revolve around children's practice schedules; even eating together becomes difficult, let alone joining together in practices and disciplines of faith.

Most children spend at least thirty hours a week in school, yet only an hour in worship and perhaps another hour or so in Sunday school or other church activities. Think about it: They return from school with homework, but the church too often acts as though children and young people will not attend its activities unless the church offers them fun and games. Family devotions have long gone out of fashion, and if family members have no time to eat together, they cannot learn to pray together before meals. If parents are to fulfill their vows to their baptized children, they will have to learn new patterns of family life and will need the support and encouragement of the wider community of faith.

My own family has struggled with these issues. When I was a child, my parents kept a short devotional time at the dinner table; as a family, we also offered prayer before meals and at bedtime. But as my siblings and I got older, our interest waned, and family schedules became more complicated. Practicing the faith was increasingly left up to each of us individually, although my parents did retain the expectation that all of us would attend Sunday worship and participate in other church activities.

In college and afterward, I made several stabs at reconnecting myself with personal disciplines of faith, but I was never able to sustain them for long; sometimes I did not even get to church. Yet I never lost the sense that I had a home in the church. Eventually I realized that I longed for the church's fellowship, and I found my way back. The church became central to my life again. I married. My wife and I had our first child, and as she grew older and approached school age, we pondered what to do. We were perhaps feeling overly protective of our firstborn, but we really did wonder how we could ever send such an innocent, precious child into the wider world. How could we help her to sustain her baptismal identity? We thought of sending her to a Christian school, or of home schooling. But in the end we concluded that every human, every member of our family too, must eventually head into a wider world; what we needed was not to avoid the world but to go into it each day with a clear sense of our common identity in Christ.

We had already established practices of prayer at meals and at bedtime. Now we added a time of morning prayer and its four basic elements of psalmody, Bible reading, hymnody, and prayer. A brief order in our denomination's *Book of Common Worship* guided us. So for the past ten years, we have gathered daily at the breakfast table and have practiced our prayers as we eat. There is nothing to romanticize in this scene. One child or another shows up late. Someone spills orange juice; someone else rummages around in the cabinets for a different kind of cereal. When school ends and we get on a summer schedule, the kids sometimes sleep late, and morning prayer falls to me and my wife. When the family goes on vacation, we seem unable to sustain morning prayer at all. Over time, we have become all too aware of how fragile our practice is, even after years of repetition.

We nevertheless continue to work at it, and in some respects, our devotional time has become richer. The children help to read the lectionary passage for the day, or to lead us in the prayer of the day. We have learned several great hymns of the faith by heart, and now the children sing them by memory in church as well. Morning prayer has become a moment of Sabbath; it flows out of and back into Sunday worship.

We do not match these practices and disciplines of the Word as intentionally with practices and disciplines of the sacraments, for the celebration of the sacraments is part of the community's worship, not a family's. But a family can direct its children to the significance of their baptism and can prepare them for participation in the Lord's Supper. How? The larger Christian church has always related baptism to the practice of confessing the faith. We should always be asking, Are we able to say what we believe? Are we growing in our knowledge of the faith? Parents have the responsibility to give their children education in the faith not only at church but also at home. Catechetical instruction of the past is suggestive today. Parents could commit themselves to seeing that their children come to know the basic documents of the faith, such as the Apostles' Creed, the Decalogue, and the Lord's Prayer.

Similarly, the church has always related the Lord's Supper to confession of sin. We again face key questions: Are we able to admit the wrong that we have inflicted on others? Are we growing in our capacity both to ask for forgiveness and to offer it? The family is an important laboratory. Over the years, my wife and I have had to learn not only to teach our children practices of reconciliation but also to ask our children for forgiveness when we have unhelpfully lost our cool with them or have failed to deliver on a promise that we had made.

Practices and disciplines of confessing faith and sin point to practices and disciplines of life together—learning, for example, to treat each other not only as family members but also as members of the body of Christ. A family may not always identify these practices and disciplines of corporate life as explicitly as did Bonhoeffer, but there is rarely a day that a Christian family will not have to think about the meaning of baptism for how it will live together. One of the most important issues in this regard is how family members learn to bear each other's burdens. How do we accommodate each other's different personalities and interests? How do we learn to see each other not only as family members but also as brothers and sisters in Christ?

There are still other family practices and disciplines that help children grow in their baptismal identity, such as celebrating their baptismal dates or including them in church service projects. But even this brief discussion suggests the key point: that for which Christian children most honor their parents is not simply physical existence and emotional well-being, but spiritual guidance and sustenance. Christian children honor Christian parents above all for baptizing, educating, and forming us in the church's faith, and for bringing us to the church's worship and helping us learn practices and disciplines that sustain us in our identity as children of the triune God.[8] Our parents have taught us submission and humility before the Lord.

Honoring Parents and Honoring God

The submission that we bring to God will call into question and redefine the submission that we owe our parents. Christian parents hope that their children will give their ultimate allegiance to God, not to them. Christian parents aim at setting their children onto their own two spiritual feet, so that their children will live in the freedom of the gospel, not in the shackles of familial relationships. The poignancy of Christian parenthood is not simply that one must give one's children wings to fly away on their own, but that one must help them to know that they have only one Father and Mother, their heavenly Parent. Every parent, like John the Baptist, must decrease, so that God in Christ might increase (John 3:30).

As Christian commentators have often noted, the tension between submission to parents and submission to God is rooted in the Gospels' account of Jesus and his family.[9] Jesus honored his parents when as a boy he returned home with them to Nazareth (Luke 2:41–51). He acceded (though not without protest!) to his mother's wishes at the wedding in Cana (John 2:1–11). Although he did not marry, he never advised men and women to reject marriage; rather, he affirmed that a man would leave his parents and be joined to his wife (Matt. 19:5). Although he had no children, he never argued against the wisdom of the Jewish tradition that the child should obey father and mother, so that the child might come to know the ways of God that they were teaching him:

My child, keep my words
  and store up my commandments with you;
keep my commandments and live,
  keep my teachings as the apple of your eye;
bind them on your fingers,
  write them on the tablet of your heart.
Prov. 7:1–3

Yet Jesus also reminded his parents that he had been in his Father's house in Jerusalem, and he spoke harsh words to his disciples about familial bonds and duties. In Matthew 8:21–22, for example, a disciple says to him, "Lord, first let me go and bury my father." Jesus replies, "Follow me, and let the dead bury their own dead." And in Matthew 10:35–37, he says, "For I have come to set a man against his father, and a daughter against her mother, and a daughter-in-law against her mother-in-law; and one's foes will be members of one's own household. Whoever loves father or mother more than me is not worthy of me." Loyalty and obedience to God redefine family bonds. So, Jesus asked, "'Who are my mother and my brothers?' And looking at those who sat around him, he said, 'Here are my mother and my brothers! Whoever does the will of God is my brother and sister and mother'" (Mark 3:33–35).

Jesus' two-sided message about family life reminds us that he never saw family values as principally a matter of good citizenship on earth. We are baptized; we are now members of God's family. Our citizenship is in heaven, even while we live on earth. The honor that Christian children owe Christian parents is first of all the honor due them for having guided us into faith. We are loyal and obedient to our parents to the extent that we are now loyal and obedient to God. For Christians, loyalty to parents may mean challenging them; submission to parents may paradoxically mean *not* submitting to them at times. If we are to be true to the baptismal identity into which our parents delivered us, we will have to resist them when they would give us identities based primarily on family heritage, nation, race, or class.

Family life profoundly shapes our identity. As we have noted, parents and children almost "naturally" train each other in submission, humility, and interdependence. These patterns of family life are not restricted to Christians, and non-Christians who practice them well may teach Christians something about the kind of family life to which God calls us. But our baptismal identity also changes our understanding of the submission, humility, and interdependence that we owe each other. Christians find significant differences between the patterns of family life that arise because parent and child naturally weigh down on each other, and the patterns of family life that arise when parent and child acknowledge each other's baptismal identity.

There is a tension between family life and baptismal identity. We have said that mutual submission is a requirement of healthy family life in general. We begin life with a greater dependence on our parents than they on us; over time this dependence becomes more mutual, until it flips over into parents' greater dependence on us. But at all times, whether we are young, middle-aged, or old, the child never simply submits to the parent, and the parent never simply submits to the child. There is always an element of mutuality. Because both parties are limited, finite beings, neither can make an absolute claim on the other, yet neither exists without a relative claim on the other. Even when one party is in a weaker position in relation to the other, the weaker party still has a right to be honored by the stronger.

This kind of mutual submission grows out of the requirements of the family's bonds. Parents attend to the crying child because it is *their* child; children grow up to be concerned about a parent because it is *their* father or mother who suffers or needs help. The family itself becomes a center of value. Father and mother may teach us about God, but almost inevitably we endow them with godlike qualities. A child may have its own life to live, but almost inevitably parents invest it with their own hopes and dreams. The mutual submission that parents and children practice tends to impose the family's identity on each member, and that identity becomes one's principal identity, especially within the family. Years later, grown adults can still feel like "children" in the presence of their parents. Parents can feel as though their children never give them the attention they deserve, even though they as parents have done so much for them.

Submission to God redefines these familial patterns of submission, humility, and interdependence. Parents claim us by virtue of giving birth to us and raising us, and we lay claim to them by reminding them of their parental responsibilities to us. By contrast, God makes *covenant* with us. In this covenantal context, God acts out of sovereign freedom. God remains the dynamic, living initiator of relationship. The submission that we owe God does not one day flip over into a submission that God owes us. God is never dependent on us. God never owes us honor. As God's creatures, we have no inherent claim on God.

Yet this covenantal relationship is not without mutuality. Even though God is not dependent on us, God nevertheless chooses to honor us. Even though we have no inherent right to God's attention, God freely allows us to weigh down on him. God does submit to us, but not as a child to a parent, not even as a parent to a child, but as the Creator and Redeemer who wishes that every parent and every child would call him "Abba." This God becomes human flesh and dies on a cross, thereby delivering us from false, sinful submission to other powers and forces of this world. This God makes a home with us. We do not have to make a home with him; we have only to enter the home that he has already prepared for us.

Life before God thus redefines life in family. Those who are baptized must obey God rather than their parents (see Acts 5:29). Our submission to God must be more emphatic, more complete, than the submission that we show a parent or any other human authority. In the words of the sixteenth-century Scots Confession, "We confess and acknowledge one God alone, to whom alone we must cleave, whom alone we must serve, whom only we must worship, and in whom alone we put our trust."[10]

Yet this submission to God teaches us a way of submission to one another that is also more profound than any family's. The God who has submitted to our human condition, who has borne it in all its sinfulness to the cross, is the God who now frees us for "grateful service to his creatures."[11] In the light of the cross, Christian parents and children see each other differently. Nature and family no longer serve as their principal bond; rather, a common baptism unites them. Parents and children now come to each other as fellow servants of the crucified and risen Christ. Each allows himself or herself to be weighed down by the parent or child, because the parent or child is now first of all a brother or sister in Christ. Thus, children best honor their parents not by celebrating Father's Day or Mother's Day, but by remembering their baptism. We submit to them not simply as father and mother, but as persons who together with us bear the mark of the Lord.

In this Christian perspective, the family members' mutual submission is reframed by their common submission to the God who has given his life for each of them. The practices and disciplines of bearing of which Bonhoeffer speaks apply equally well to a family that discovers its center in Jesus Christ:

> "Bear one another's burdens, and in this way you will fulfill the law of Christ" (Gal. 6:2). . . . Christians must bear the burden of one another. They must suffer and endure one another. Only as a burden is the other really a brother or sister and not just an object to be controlled. The burden of human beings was even for God so heavy that God had to go to the cross suffering under it. God truly suffered and endured human beings in the body of Jesus Christ. But in so

> doing, God bore them as a mother carries her child, as a shepherd the lost lamb. God took on human nature. Then, human beings crushed God to the ground. But God stayed with them and they with God. In suffering and enduring human beings, God maintained community with them. . . . Now by virtue of the law of Christ having been fulfilled, [Christians] are also able to bear one another.[12]

So loyalty and obedience to God may at times require us not to break family bonds but, rather, to shape a deeper relationship with our parents. God may ask us as Christians to give more of ourselves to our families than ever before. Jesus criticized those who proclaimed the fifth commandment with their mouths but then turned around and said to father or mother, "'Whatever support you might have had from me is Corban' (that is, an offering to God) . . . thus making void the word of God" (Mark 7:11–13).

Our Christian calling may require us to submit to our parents in new, unexpected ways. To grow in relationship with God will almost surely mean that God asks us to grow into fuller interdependency with others, including our parents. But the character of this interdependency will have changed. It is now "in the Lord." Being brothers and sisters in Christ now teaches us what it means to be brothers and sisters, parents and children, in families. We learn to bear the burdens of each family member as a practice and discipline not just of family life but also of our shared Christian faith.

The tension between honoring God and honoring parents has sometimes been acutely experienced by children whose Christian calling led them to faraway places, where they would rarely if ever see their parents again. Such a story has been handed down in my family. My great-grandfather Burgess left England in the 1870s to become a missionary to Turkey. After only a few months in the field, he contracted tuberculosis and had to return home. He passed the remainder of his short life searching for drier, cleaner air. First he immigrated to the United States, where he married a Jewish woman from New York City (a grandniece of Solomon Heine!). Then began a great trek westward; their first child was born in New York, the second in Ohio, the third in Kansas, and the fourth in Colorado, where my great-grandfather died at age thirty-three, leaving my great-grandmother to raise their four young children in a small town on the Rocky Mountain frontier. My great-grandparents had named their eldest son Paul, praying that he would someday fulfill the missionary call that his father could not. Paul for his part seems never to have doubted that he would become a missionary. After completing seminary, he and his wife volunteered for mission service with the Presbyterian Church (U.S.A.) and were assigned to the Indian highlands of Guatemala, in Central America, where they would spend their adult lives and be buried.[13]

Paul had a special relationship with his mother, and they loved to talk about intellectual topics. I once found in the old family home in Cañon City, Colorado, a book that Paul had given his mother on her fortieth birthday: the collected works of Plato! He had been the eldest son, the one to whom surely his mother had looked when her husband died. But Paul's move to Guatemala meant that he saw her only sporadically in the following years. Their love was as deep as ever; whenever he visited home after several years' absence, the conversations on her back porch went long into the night. But submission to what both understood to be the will of God required that they thoroughly reweave the fabric of interdependency that held them together. They continued to hold each other close but had to rely on letters and sporadic visits rather than daily rhythms of life together.

Adult children often live far away from their parents, drawn by the requirements of a career or a marriage. Parent and child may then have less time in each other's presence and be less able to care for each other on a daily basis. As difficult as these changes are, they need not weaken or destroy the relationship. On the contrary, parent and child may long for each other more deeply. Their lives may become weightier to each other. They may increasingly sense their responsibility to support each other in their baptismal identity.

Family members' most profound moments of holding each other in thought and prayer may occur when the child becomes old enough to realize that his parents will die someday—and old enough that the parents realize that their child, their baby and precious one, will someday die too. Parent and child wonder to themselves where home will then be if someday they are the one left, having only memories but not the dear one whom they loved so deeply.

The Comprehensive Implications of the Commandment

The fifth commandment summons Christian parents and children to a distinctive way of life before God. Christian children will honor their parents by remembering all that they have done for us, and especially by giving thanks and praise for all that they have done to remind us who we are as children of the triune God. But these practices and disciplines must evolve over time; the family relationship must grow into a Christian relationship. Together, parents and children must uphold each other in bonds of Christian faith and love, and their mutual honoring must lead them into a deeper understanding of the commandment and its requirements.

The three interpretive moves that I explored in chapter 2 also apply here: The commandment must be reversed, related to inner motivations, and understood as a broad category. When we reverse the commandment, we remember that honoring parents requires us *not* to honor any of their actions that would lead us away from our baptismal identity. Honoring parents, as we have seen, may at times mean opposing them, even calling them back to their true identity in Christ. When we discover the deeper meaning of the fifth commandment, we realize that honoring parents does not cover up but rather lays bare the real struggles that ensue whenever a family works together to give its greatest honor to God, not to itself.

In reversing the commandment, we also remember that we should do nothing to diminish the significance of our parents. We will refuse to dishonor them even when we disagree with them, even when we have suffered under their authority. If our parents have not been the parents they should have been, we will nevertheless honor them as best we can, especially if they helped direct us to our Christian identity—even if they did nothing more than baptize us.

The commandment is as applicable to our inner attitudes as to our outer behaviors. Honoring parents is then not just a matter of keeping them satisfied or meeting cultural expectations (an occasional telephone call, a card on their birthday, or whatever else society recommends), but of letting their lives weigh down on us—that is, of letting their burdens, frustrations, and hopes *affect* us. To honor our parents means to have feelings toward them, to care about them and to forbear them, to worry about them and to hope that they worry about us. Their lives will matter to us; we will have a sense of their life's weightiness—but now not just as father and mother but also as brother and sister in Christ.

The comprehensive implications of the commandment become most apparent when we broaden it and think of parents as a *category*, not just as two individuals. The African proverb, "It takes a village to raise a child," reminds us that many people help to sustain our lives; every baptized Christian needs the support not only of parents but also of the wider community of faith to help him or her to grow in faith. As children in the faith, we owe honor to all those spiritual parents who have reminded us who we really are in Christ. Calvin spoke eloquently of the church as the mother that nurtures us in the faith.[14] Even with its faults, divisions, and scandals, the church should command our submission and humility—but here too, ultimately for the sake of interdependence "in the Lord."

The church, like Christian families, needs to develop practices and disciplines of mutual submission. We especially need forms of church discipline that help us encourage and hold each other accountable in the faith. Most North American Christians, like their secular counterparts, think first in terms of personal interests and political posturing, even in the church. We have a difficult time knowing what it means to be the body of Christ. We still need to learn how to keep ourselves rooted in Word and sacrament, and how to bear each other's burdens.

When the church today does think of discipline, it is too often influenced by the litigious spirit of American society. Discipline becomes primarily a matter of church trials and penalties. But such discipline threatens to become merely punitive and even sinfully distorted, an assertion of human interests against each other, unless it is grounded in a richer sense of discipline as life together.[15]

As the Christian tradition has broadened the fifth commandment, it has allowed it to reach beyond the sphere of the family and the church. Particular emphasis has fallen on political authorities. Christians have sometimes seen parallels between parents and the parental rule of the state. The fifth commandment has been used to justify political submission—but political resistance as well, when political authorities have failed to execute justice.[16]

Superior, Inferior, or Equal?

Here, however, I am interested in a different move that the Christian tradition has made. The Westminster Larger Catechism of the seventeenth century understands the fifth commandment to refer not only to what subjects owe authorities but also to what authorities owe subjects, and to what social equals owe each other (qq. 127–32). This way of broadening the commandment draws us into the full complexity of human relationships.

The Larger Catechism thinks of a world in which social position is set and relatively unalterable. One is born a ruler or a subject or an equal in relation to others. Parents rule over children, parents and children together are subject to political rulers, and parents have social equals, as do their children. The reality in our day is more complicated. As we have already noted in relation to families, children begin life in the more submissive role but quickly grow up and become their parents' equals. Eventually, they may even "rule" over their aging parents, making decisions on their behalf. Parents and children then exchange roles. Similarly, our larger social relationships evolve. Rulers may suddenly be cast down from their thrones, while the lowly are lifted up (Luke 2:52), or those once divided by race or class may come to discover their shared humanity and their essential equality.

Christians' baptismal identity further complicates the picture. In coming to know who we really are, we also believe that we know others' true identity, whether they are baptized or not. God seeks relationship with every human being—relationship characterized by the intimacy of Jesus Christ with his "brothers and sisters." We cannot look at another without seeing him or her as a child of God, for whom Christ died and to whom the living Christ calls. Christian practices of mutual submission suggest that we will always relate to others, both inside and outside the church, in all three modes—submission, rule, and equality—simultaneously.

In some respects, the other is always our "ruler." He or she has talents and abilities that command our respect and honor. The other plays the piano with beauty, or is a superb mechanic, or has great patience and capacity to be emotionally present to others. There is no human being who in one way or another is not our superior. But, conversely, there is no human being who cannot in some respects learn from us—from our particular history, experience, natural abilities, or acquired skills. We are never inferior or superior to another absolutely, but only relatively. We need each other, despite our differences.

An egalitarian society emphasizes our equality, especially our equal rights before the law. But the mutual submission that we learn in families, and more fully in Christ, teaches us that true interdependence grows out of our differing abilities, and therefore out of the variety of ways in which we complement and correct each other. What is true of our natural condition is even truer of our spiritual condition. Spiritually, we will interrelate in complex patterns of submission and rule. Others will commandingly call us back to our baptismal identity, just as at times we will call them. The apostle Paul speaks of the way that the Spirit has distributed different gifts (1 Cor. 12). We are never simply equals in the faith. We have specific roles to play that make us interdependent, precisely because others have spiritual gifts and insights that we need, just as we have gifts and insights that they need.

Our baptismal identity does nevertheless allow us to see each other not only as superiors/inferiors but also as equals. Christians affirm the equality that a democratic political order secures. We affirm the inherent equality that all humans share by virtue of having been created by God and sharing the human condition, with its sinfulness as well as its longings for redemption. But we know of yet another kind of equality, one more profound than that bestowed by politics or nature—the equality of those who stand before the living God. We see others as those whom God has given us for the journey of life in Christ. With those who affirm their baptismal identity, we share particular joys and responsibilities—life in the church. But even those outside the church are our partners. We long for them to know their true identity, and we give thanks to God for ways in which God uses them unwittingly to sustain us.

The comprehensive implications of the fifth commandment call us to practices and disciplines of faith that enable us to grow into deeper interdependence, whether in families, in the church, or in society. We work at discovering our places of dependence, authority, and equality in all relationships, seeking finally to bear each other's burdens—to give honor and to be honored, to be weighed down and to be of weight, to stand apart from and yet together with others as children of the God who is Father, Son, and Holy Spirit. We come to see each other's unique gifts and to acknowledge the ways in which others serve as "father" or "mother" to us, or we to them. But we also see "father" and "mother" as the brother and sister with whom we share a common baptismal identity. We practice seeing each other as God sees us—weak, helpless babies in whom God nevertheless takes delight.

When Relationship Is Broken

When the world runs only on the principle of competitive self-assertion, it becomes violently chaotic.[17] People can live together only to the degree that they nurture the rich and complex ways in which each person is simultaneously inferior, superior, and equal to others. We can develop bonds of trust and cooperation only as we acquire a deep capacity for patience and forgiveness, for self-restraint and courageous intervention. At the point that either family or public life becomes characterized by indifference, its very fabric is unraveling.

Living together takes practice and discipline because it is not easy. Members of a community not only complement each other but also get in each other's way. The weightiness of another person's life sometimes makes us feel honored; other times it threatens to crush us. Life in family or society can become sinfully distorted. As a result, allowing the other to weigh me down may not be an act of honor. God does not ask us to carry every burden. Some burdens must be challenged, even refused.

Christian children and Christian parents live rightly with each other only as they receive strength from beyond themselves and grow in the new life that Jesus Christ alone makes possible. Along this difficult road, every Christian must learn to abandon father and mother (or son and daughter), in order to receive them back as brother and sister in Christ.

In truth, this transition does not always take place. Parents who have their children baptized do not always know how to let go of them, or how to respect and nurture their baptismal identity. Children who have been baptized do not always remain in the church. To work at becoming not merely parent and child but also brother and sister in Christ sometimes brings as much disappointment as joy.

Practices and disciplines of faith guarantee nothing. The family that prays together does not necessarily stay together. Family devotions at home and attendance at church do not by themselves make us Christian. Practices and disciplines of faith are marvelous pathways that God's Spirit regularly uses to remind us of our baptismal identity, but they do not dispense drops of miracle "faith-grow." Practices and disciplines make sense only to the degree that we participate in them freely, out of a profound sense of gratitude for the gift of faith in Jesus Christ, even as they nurture this sense of gratitude.

What happens when Christian parent and Christian child do not become brother or sister in Christ? Whenever a parent and a child break bonds, having nothing more to do with each other, deep pain results. The anguish of a parent (or child) is often compounded when a child (or parent), baptized and raised in the church, turns away from the church. Patterns of familial interdependence may not dissolve entirely. Parent and child may still see each other, may still enjoy each other's company. But they really have headed in different directions, with different identities, rather than with a shared baptismal identity. Wonderfully yet tragically, a Christian may come to have a much deeper sense of family with his or her friends in the faith than with his or her own children (or parents).

Even in these situations, practices and disciplines of faith can continue to play a profound role. The Christian parent (or child) always has reason to hold the baptized child (or parent) in prayer, because the one knows the other's true identity in Christ. Children may strike out on their own, implicitly or explicitly rejecting their baptismal identity, but the parent knows in his or her heart who the child really is. A Christian parent will always live in prayerful hope for a baptized child, even when he or she has wandered away from the church. The parent's anguish does not go away, but as father or mother one seeks to nurture whatever patterns of interdependence with the child that are still possible, as weak and remote as they may appear.

The Christian parent who has had a child baptized has placed that child in the hands of God. Father and mother will do whatever they can to remind their child of its Trinitarian name—and if it comes to the point that they can do nothing more than pray, even then they will seek to honor the child, allowing its life to weigh upon them. They will hold their son or daughter in their minds and hearts, knowing that their child has a place in God's heart. Even a child who wanders away from home should know that it always has a home to which it can return.[18]

Going Home

"Honor your father and your mother, so that your days may be long in the land that the LORD your God is giving you." Home is never simply a piece of land or a particular landscape. Home is the country lanes that we have walked with good friends, or the dark, musty schoolroom in which a teacher showed special care for us, or the redbrick house on a quiet, shaded street, in which we lived together as a family and where our mother kept her books on old green shelves or our father helped us drive our play automobiles on the living room rug with its blocks and swirls of color.

Once we have left, a return trip to the old family homestead does not necessarily get us back home, even though it may momentarily offer a free zone for a lot of rich reminiscing. Home is as much a verb as a noun. It is something that *happens*—and it can happen only with and through *people* who care for us, encourage us, give us life, and allow us to love them. Only as we honor these "parents" can we find our way home.[19]

As the apostle Paul noted (Eph. 6:2), the fifth commandment is the first (and only) of the Ten Commandments with a promise: "that your days may be long in the land that the LORD your God is giving you." Christian theologians have sometimes put the emphasis on living *long*. They have of course known that dutiful children do not necessarily live a longer span of years than those who despise their parents, for "he makes his sun rise on the evil and on the good, and sends rain on the righteous and the unrighteous" (Matt. 5:45). But they have typically solved this problem by interpreting the word "long" spiritually rather than literally. They have argued that those who honor their parents will live a better life here and now and will be fitter for the heavenly life to come.

Yet I do not want to lose the concrete, this-worldly, topographical significance of the fifth commandment. The promise is not simply *long*, but *in the land*. How do we finally come to feel at home in one place or another? I believe that home happens as particular places become bound up in our memories with particular people, such as the places where I walked with my mother on that early spring day and that she associated with her parents. Even more clearly, home is the place where people continue to shape life together, and where memory is not simply a reaching back into the past but also a reaching forward into the future, as people affirm and support each other in their true identity before God.

There is no need to romanticize family life. Not every family recognizes or sustains its members' God-given identities and deserves to be called a home. Moreover, making home is not limited to families and to the life that parents and children make together. But many Christians have grown up in a family that did give them sustenance for life's journey—whatever deficiencies it had—and many of us have become parents and have tried, despite our own faults and limitations, to care for our children and to guide them into God's future. So it was in a family, with our parents, that most of us first came to sense where and what our home was.

We may spend the rest of our lives trying to get back to the home that we once knew, or looking for what we think would be a better home than the one we once had. But there is another possibility. By God's grace, we may shape home anew *with* our parents, as they and we grow older. This true home is the home that Jesus Christ has made with us. It is the heavenly kingdom in which father and mother and son and daughter are all children, for "whoever does not receive the kingdom of God as a little child will never enter it" (Mark 10:15). We are sons and daughters of the triune God and therefore brothers and sisters to each other.

Long ago, a newborn baby was handed from one pair of hands to another. Questions were asked; a name was given. That baby was returned to his parents, but he no longer belonged to them. Nearly fifty years ago, my parents were courageous enough to let go of me. Ever since, they have been faithful enough to let my life—my baptismal identity—weigh upon them. I have given them reason for praise and thanksgiving, sorrow and supplication.

I have already had to let go of my father, and a day will come, sooner than I would ever wish or imagine, when that little baby, now a middle-aged, balding man, will also have to hand his mother over from this world to the next. The loving hands that once caressed him as a baby will lie quietly at her side. The lips that once reminded him who he really was will no longer move. He will now simply have to entrust her into the hands of God, knowing that she no longer belongs to him—that she never belonged to him but has always been God's child.

At that funeral service, no questions will be asked, but a precious name will again be spoken:

> In sure and certain hope of the resurrection to eternal life,
> through the Lord Jesus Christ,
> we commend to almighty God our sister Elizabeth Anne,
> and we commit her body to the ground,
> earth to earth, ashes to ashes, dust to dust.
>
> In her baptism she was clothed with Christ;
> in the day of Christ's coming,
> she shall be clothed with glory.[20]

Chapter Five

Facing the World

You shall not murder.
Exod. 20:13

The *New York Times* recently ran a series on the Ten Commandments.[1] I might not have been surprised had I been reading the Lincoln *Journal Star* or the Mobile *Register* or a small-town, local newspaper that still prints a Scripture verse of the day on its front page. But I did not expect to read about the commandments in the *Times*. To me, the *Times* represents secular, pluralistic America at its best—intelligent, open-minded, and socially progressive. Wouldn't the editors of the *Times* find the Ten Commandments embarrassingly parochial and legalistic, the specific legacy of Jews and Christians and their checkered past?

The writer plumbed the commandments for the wisdom that people continue to find in them, even some who have been profoundly shaped by a secular, pluralistic culture. Perhaps unconsciously, he demonstrated what Jews and Christians themselves have often claimed: that the commandments point to truths about the *human* condition. Jews and Christians have wanted to embody the way of life that the commandments describe, not just for the sake of their own salvation but also for the sake of the world. They have wanted to say, Look, here is the fundamental moral order that defines the grain of the universe.

The article on the fourth commandment noted ways in which people are rediscovering Sabbath, as they set aside a day in which they can slow down, gather with family and friends, and meditate on the greater mystery of their lives. The piece on the fifth commandment described a young man who had sought to honor the memory of his father, a U.S.

Army helicopter pilot who had died in combat in El Salvador. After years of anger and depression, the young man had entered West Point and become a soldier himself.

But what moved me most deeply was the treatment of the sixth commandment, "Do not kill."[2] The *Times* told the story of an Episcopal priest who had become a military chaplain. As a young man, he had served in an elite commando unit in Vietnam. The army, he would later say, had done its work well. He had learned to be a killer. He had killed not just once, but again and again. He had seen movies in which soldiers vomited in revulsion after their first experience of killing. But he himself had never felt anything. He simply did his job as effectively and efficiently as possible.

Or did he feel *something*? Whenever he killed a Vietnamese soldier, he was supposed to search the body. Sometimes he would find pictures, notes, or other reminders of a parent, wife, or child. One day he found a small, square photograph of a beautiful blond American woman, probably removed by that Vietnamese soldier from a dead American's body. He slowly began to realize that each of these bodies had belonged to a unique individual, with a life like his own.

After the war, troubled by what he had experienced, he entered seminary. As he wrestled with what the Bible and Christian theology had to say about war and peace, he slowly came to a sense of inner resolution, though not by becoming a pacifist or an angry opponent of U.S. military power. Even as a Christian, he concluded that war might sometimes be necessary. Something like a "just war" might indeed exist. Christian faith did not rule out all use of force. But he was concerned about those whom we as a nation ask to be killers. He worried about the young men and women who find themselves pulling a trigger and blowing a body to bits. He knew what the state, the media, and most of us don't want to know: that you can't kill another person, not even in the name of a righteous cause, without doing something awful to yourself. He knew how desperately soldiers need a minister—someone who will pray with them and stand by them as they serve their country.

The Question of Responsibility

More than four centuries ago, John Calvin wrote that war inevitably pollutes its actors. "Although an enemy is killed in open war and God forgives it, provided the man who kills has a just and lawful cause and does so out of necessity, nevertheless the fact remains . . . that the man is soiled."[3] The killer violates himself, not only his victim. Killing strikes at the very heart of our identity, because God created us to be in relationship with each other and so to uphold and support each other.[4] Every man and woman is our neighbor and is of "our flesh." Others "must be dear and precious to us."[5] Even the enemy who poses an immediate threat to us is nevertheless a fellow human who is entrusted to our care. To take another person's life is to take something out of one's own life.

Yet, as American philosopher J. Glenn Gray remarked during the Vietnam era, most soldiers successfully evade a sense of responsibility for their actions. They view themselves as caught up in powers and forces beyond their personal control. They are "only doing their job." War teaches the soldier to repress his conscience. Moreover, the propaganda that drives contemporary warfare typically represents the enemy as so barbaric and so fully an incarnation of radical evil that the enemy is no longer human and therefore no longer worthy of humanity or humane treatment. Only occasionally does a soldier's conscience awaken to the ache of guilt—and then he often finds that he must pursue a lonely journey of anguished reflection (and sometimes of repentance before an Almighty God) that to many of those around him is incomprehensible.[6]

War starkly poses the moral dilemmas of man's inhumanity to man. But the problem of war and killing lies not only at the personal level of the combatant. If contemporary warfare makes a sense of personal responsibility more evasive, it also makes the question of collective responsibility more pressing. Especially in a democratic society, every citizen bears a measure of responsibility for the state's decisions.[7] We have the opportunity to choose our leaders and to make our opinions known to them. Presidents can rarely wage war without widespread public support. More significantly, a democracy presupposes that its citizens share a sense of participating in a common enterprise. We share a responsibility to make the good society together.

Like the combatant, the citizen may dispute the idea that he or she ultimately bears responsibility for the decisions of leaders in Washington, whom he or she usually knows only as media creations. We rail at politicians, calling them crooks and charlatans. Or we become indifferent about voting. Or we refuse to see elected leaders as representing us personally, because after all we did not vote for them. (Think of the bumper sticker that appeared after Bill Clinton's election: "Don't blame me, I voted for Bush.") But the notion of collective responsibility still manages to come home in dramatic and disturbing ways, such as when we venture abroad and discover that others regard us as representatives of the nation and its policies.

I think of my first trip overseas, in 1979. I was a young American, just out of college, and was traveling to West Germany, a country that had put aside its Nazi legacy and had become a staunch ally of the United States. But Germans were also wary of the American military presence. In the mid-'70s, the United States had begun installing medium-range missiles in West Germany, aimed at the East Bloc—a move that aroused great controversy. Large protest demonstrations took place, especially at the major German universities, as in Heidelberg, where I was living. One wintry day I walked by an elementary school. My down jacket, not typical attire in those days for a German, gave me away as an American. A group of young boys began taunting me, "Ami, go home." At that moment and subsequently, I felt no personal responsibility for NATO decisions. Yet somehow I had come to represent them to these German school kids. University students sometimes made the same association and would ask me to explain America's position on various political issues.

Was I in some sense guilty for the actions of my nation? Surely the notion of collective guilt is complex, and we must think in terms of degrees of guilt and exoneration. Not every German was responsible in the same way for the Holocaust; some saved Jews, a few even engaged in conspiratorial actions. Not every American bears the same measure of responsibility for the war in Vietnam, the Cold War, or, as I write, the occupation of Iraq.

Yet, as philosopher Gray suggests, a thoughtful German or American will sense that his personal identity is not entirely separable from the nation's. He will experience the actions of the nation, past and present, as sources of pride or shame, precisely because he has some elusive sense that he belongs to it, even if the nation by itself never fully defines who he is. My young tormentors reminded me that I really was an American (even if that stupid down coat hadn't given me away!). Ironically, they made me feel more defensive of my country than I might have felt otherwise.

Similar complexities attend relations between the races and between men and women. Social location shapes a person's sense of identity. Specific social factors that we did not entirely choose inevitably influence whether we benefit from distinct privileges and opportunities socially, or suffer under specific prejudices and inequalities. We are never entirely able to escape the impact of class, gender, nationality, and other social identities on who we are and what we can do with life, even if we can learn to become more aware and critical of their influence. These social identities burden us, yet to some degree, if Gray is correct, a thoughtful person ends up claiming them as his or her own and comes to feel a measure of responsibility for what others of his or her class, gender, or nationality do.

This social shaping of the self expands traditional Christian notions of sin.[8] Social factors inevitably influence what we take to be in our own self-interest; they also compound our difficulty in considering others' perspectives. As Christians, we know that class, gender, and nationality do not constitute our true identity, which is in Christ. We nevertheless find ourselves having to acknowledge just how much these socially created and socially bestowed identities hold us captive. We can never simply renounce them once and for all, as though we could be "generic" Christians. Self-examination and repentance of sin become all the more difficult when we realize that our sins are never simply personal but also have this social, corporate dimension.

The *New York Times* article on the sixth commandment raised the painful question of what happens to the psyche (might we say "soul" or "identity"?) of those who kill on behalf of the nation. But we could also pose the question in terms of what is violated in those of us *on whose behalf* soldiers kill. In what sense does each of us participate, however inadvertently or remotely, in the soldier's actions? In what ways are all of us caught up in larger webs of social life that implicate us in killing? And what happens to the soul of a nation that regularly resorts to force to get its way? How do individual citizens experience (or not experience) an ache of guilt for the wars that their nation wages?[9]

I did not support the American war against Saddam Hussein in 2003. I suppose that I might claim a clear conscience. Yet the actions of the nation burdened me—not only because they violated my sense of right but also because they exposed my entanglement with the victors. I cannot escape the sense that I too went to war on the American side, whether I wanted to or not. I shared in its spoils; I shared in its ravages and failures.

I am burdened by the fact that despite my doubts about the legitimacy of the war, I nevertheless hoped that the American victory would be swift and overwhelming. I am burdened by the fact that the American media (and therefore the American people, myself included) gave far greater attention to the names and stories and families of the several hundred American service personnel who were killed in the first weeks of action than to the several thousand Iraqi soldiers and civilians who died as victims of American bombs and bullets. I am burdened by the fact that no American is entirely able to resist the hope that his or her nation is ultimately engaged in a righteous cause, however many mistakes it makes along the way. I did not choose the war. Yet, in a sense, it chose me and every other American, with implications that we are still trying to unravel.

Perhaps most Americans, myself included, will quickly forget these questions of a somewhat troubled conscience. After all, life goes on; the day's troubles are sufficient for the day. But one cannot help but wonder what the war has said about us as a nation. Did it deepen our commitment to promoting and preserving life? Did it deepen bonds of international friendship? Will the peoples of the earth live in a more secure peace? Or will we as a nation simply suffer from greater hubris? Will we do what every empire does and assume that what secures our interests is in the best interest of the rest of the globe? Even if we conclude that the war was in some sense just, how has it nevertheless soiled us? What damage has it done to our identity as a people? And if it was not just, what have we betrayed in ourselves by waging it? What judgment of God or the nations do we await or have we perhaps already brought upon ourselves?

A citizen's sense of implicitly participating in acts of killing beyond himself or herself is especially marked in the case of war. But a person may also experience a sense of responsibility for other forms of social violence. One of the most controversial and emotional issues of our day is abortion. A nation actively wages war; it only *allows* a woman to make up her own mind about an abortion. Yet, even here, social policies end up implicating all of us, for better or worse. I am among those who believe that abortion should be legally available, even if with restriction. Yet it also seems to me that abortion is a form of killing, although I do not raise it to the level of first-degree murder. A fertilized embryo is more than just a random collection of cells—rather, it represents the beginning of a human life—and at later stages, the burgeoning humanity of the fetus demands ever greater respect and care. A citizen such as I may see no alternative to legalized abortion yet may simultaneously be troubled by the fact that a desire to preserve the integrity of the mother's life clashes with preserving a new human life that is still weak and just beginning.

At stake for society is not simply the morality of any particular abortion, but what abortion, when widely practiced, says about society and our sense of life together. What social forces account for the fact that one out of every four pregnancies in the United States is aborted? How does the widespread availability of abortion change the way each of us, whether foe or proponent, thinks about sexuality and procreation? What does abortion as a social phenomenon do to people's sense of the value and worth of life in general? Abortion is not only a question of personal decision making under difficult, tragic circumstances; it is also a question of the social fabric that holds us together.

Similar questions arise in relation to other forms of social violence, whether legally sanctioned (such as capital punishment), implicitly tolerated (such as poverty), or legally and morally condemned, though not always effectively combated (such as domestic abuse).[10] Wherever violence and killing occur (with the possible exception of freak accidents), there are contributing factors that inevitably reflect larger social realities and processes in which we participate, from which we benefit, and under which we suffer.

No one needs to bear excessive personal guilt for any of these complex social phenomena. Yet none of us should be afraid to ask what these phenomena mean for the health and integrity of the society in which we live. Calvin was right: We are bound one to the other. We are fundamentally social creatures, created to reach out to each other in love. Socially conditioned violence hurts all of us—not only because we share in the pain of the victim but also because we share in the guilt of the victimizer, or at least in the ache of guilt that he or she experiences.

As philosopher Gray would remind us, the human conscience manages in most cases to remain complacent. The Episcopal army chaplain would surely tell us as well that many soldiers never seek out the church's ministry. Apparently, soldiers who kill do not always ache inside. Or if they do, they do not often make much of it—just as few of us dwell for long on our occasional pangs of social guilt and responsibility for what the soldier has done. The troubled conscience, whether the killer's or the citizen's, is quickly diverted by the cares and worries and headlines of the next day.[11]

Nevertheless, Christians believe that the conscience can and should be awakened, so that the self might be converted. Even now, Christ calls us to repent of specific social idolatries that would define our lives. The troubled conscience need not paralyze us. In Christ, it can stir us to shape a different world. We cannot easily change larger social policies or attitudes about war, abortion, capital punishment, or other forms of violence. But we can commit ourselves to work for social conditions that promote deeper respect for life, beginning in the smaller circles of family, friends, and neighbors in which we participate.

The new life in Christ asks us to separate ourselves from an evil world.

Yet, in another sense, it drives us back into the world. In the light of Christ's mercy, we see just how much we are related to the world. Its capacity for evil is our own. Its sins, as we have seen, weigh upon us. Too often we ourselves have contributed to the world's problems, sometimes consciously (sins of commission), other times by failing to act with greater boldness (sins of omission). Moreover, Christians know that sin goes beyond dynamics of class, gender, or nationality; "original sin" lies at the very heart of the human condition: "They have all gone astray, they are all alike perverse; there is no one who does good, no, not one" (Ps. 14:3). "All, both Jews and Greeks, are under the power of sin" (Rom. 3:9).

Sin places us in solidarity with the world. But the new life in Christ also sends us into another, more profound kind of solidarity with the world. Life in Christ is . . . life . . . under the cross . . . with others. I allow others and their actions to weigh me down. I no longer see myself in isolation from others, or my actions apart from theirs. God's will to redeem the whole of creation draws me into the world. I face it; I take responsibility for it, even for those sins that are not mine. I join with Christian brothers and sisters in interceding for a violated, violating world, offering it up to God for God's transforming grace.

Scripture speaks again and again of bearing: "Bear one another's burdens" (Gal. 6:2). "Bear with one another and, if anyone has a complaint against another, forgive each other" (Col. 3:13). "Be kind to one another, tenderhearted, forgiving one another, as God in Christ has forgiven you" (Eph. 4:32). This bearing, as I have suggested, begins in the Christian household (both in family and in the church!). It trains us for life in the world so that we might take on what is perhaps the greatest burden of all: to forgive our enemies. In Christ, I allow even the enemy to weigh me down—to become *human* in my sight, a fellow bearer of the image of God, a child called like me to know the God who is Father, Son, and Holy Spirit. I face the enemy and now acknowledge that he or she too has a face.[12]

Expanding the Commandment

No society can long endure unless its members cultivate an ever greater sense of personal and social responsibility. From a Christian perspective, we need practices and disciplines that make life with each other more possible, beginning with the life of the church. The three interpretive strategies that I have applied to the fourth and fifth commandments—

broadening, internalizing, and reversing—also apply here. In its comprehensive form, the sixth commandment speaks not only to the discrete act of taking another person's life but also to the broader dilemmas of the troubled conscience. Jesus' Sermon on the Mount provides a basis for proceeding in this way:

> You have heard that it was said to those of ancient times, "You shall not murder"; and "whoever murders shall be liable to judgment." But I say to you that if you are angry with a brother or sister, you will be liable to judgment; and if you insult a brother or sister, you will be liable to the council; and if you say, "You fool," you will be liable to the hell of fire. So when you are offering your gift at the altar, if you remember that your brother or sister has something against you, leave your gift there before the altar and go; first be reconciled to your brother or sister, and then come and offer your gift. (Matt. 5:21–24)

As we see, Jesus first *broadens* the commandment into a category of behavior. "Murder" happens not only with weapons but also with words. Like a blow to the head, an insult or a curse can leave lasting wounds. Similarly, the labels that we place on people and the assumptions that we make about them can long debilitate them. Sticks and stones can break my bones—and words can hurt me too.

Second, Jesus expands the commandment to apply to *inner attitudes*. "Do not kill" means that we should not even be angry with a brother or sister. Even if our anger does not come spilling out as destructive words and actions, it keeps us from embracing our neighbor. Our internal life inevitably shapes our external behavior.

Third, Jesus *reverses* the commandment, making the negative into a positive. "Do not kill" also means that we should work for reconciliation with those who are estranged from us. The sixth commandment calls us into a deeper love of neighbor, a love shaped by the cross. It is not enough for us to leave the neighbor alone; as Christians, we are also called to protect and promote his or her life.

The Heidelberg Catechism provides a noteworthy example of how the Christian tradition has developed these interpretive moves. The catechism first establishes the broad scope of the commandment: "I am not to abuse, hate, injure, or kill my neighbor, either with thought, or by word or gesture, much less by deed, whether by myself or through another, but to lay aside all desire for revenge" (q. 105). Next it notes the commandment's internal dimension: "In forbidding murder God means to teach us that he abhors the root of murder, which is envy, hatred, anger, and desire for revenge, and that he regards all these as hidden murder" (q. 106).

Finally, the catechism asks, "Is it enough, then, if we do not kill our neighbor in any of these ways?" It says, "No," and then turns the negative into a positive: "When God condemns envy, hatred, and anger, he requires us to love our neighbors as ourselves, to show patience, peace, gentleness, mercy, and friendliness toward him, to prevent injury to him as much as we can, also to do good to our enemies" (q. 107). The "thou shalt not" also implies a "thou shalt": Promote the well-being of the neighbor.

The Westminster Larger Catechism represents the full flowering of these interpretive possibilities in the Reformed tradition. Significantly, the catechism lists the positive duties of the commandment prior to "the sins forbidden." In both cases, the commandment then develops extensive lists of actions and dispositions. The catechism's injunctions and prohibitions are best understood not as exhaustive checklists but as suggestive examples of the scope of the commandment as it reaches into every area of life. The listing under "duties required" is illustrative:

> All careful studies and lawful endeavors, to preserve life of ourselves and others, by resisting all thoughts and purposes, subduing all passions, and avoiding all occasions, temptations, and practices, which tend to the unjust taking of life of any; by just defense thereof against violence; patient bearing of the hand of God, quietness of mind, cheerfulness of recreation; by charitable thoughts, love, compassion, meekness, gentleness, kindness, peaceable, mild, and courteous speeches and behavior, forbearance, readiness to be reconciled, patient bearing and forgiving injuries, and requiting good for evil; comforting and succoring the distressed, and protecting and defending the innocent. (q. 135)

These strategies for broadening the sixth commandment point to the close relationship among all the commandments of the second table. "Do not commit adultery," "Do not steal," "Do not bear false witness," and "Do not covet" can all be understood as explications of "Do not kill/promote and protect life." They expand the scope of the sixth commandment and therefore of the key practices and disciplines that shape and sustain Christian love for the neighbor.[13] The seventh commandment, for example, is not only about sex outside of marriage. More fundamentally, it is about maintaining integrity in all relationships, beginning with marriage. The trust and faithfulness that are necessary for a marriage to thrive are equally essential in society. We cannot live long or well unless we are able to rely on the people around us.

Similarly, the eighth commandment is not only about keeping my hands off my neighbor's property. It also reminds us that we cannot live long or well unless we give each other space. Each of us needs to know that our existence is respected, no matter what our race, gender, or class; that others recognize and honor our particular gifts and talents, no matter what our limitations; and that others need us and will care for us if we become unable to care for ourselves. The eighth commandment summons us to practice justice both by protecting what belongs rightfully to others and by giving others their due.

The ninth commandment is not only about words that slander others. Not bearing false witness also requires me to speak truthfully about my neighbor. I must refrain from destructive gossip—but also from self-serving flattery. I must not stereotype others, but I must also not fail to acknowledge their backgrounds and the specific social factors (such as race, gender, and class) that have helped to make them who they are.[14] I am honest, yet I do not use the truth to put others down. As a discipline of love, Christian truth-telling is finally in the service of strengthening human relationships and honoring others as children of God.[15]

The tenth commandment drives home the inner transformation that all the commandments require. The inner self must be shaped by God's love, rather than by personal self-centeredness. To covet what belongs to the other is to live without regard for him or her. Conversely, not to covet requires me to work for the good of my neighbor, even at expense to myself.

In sum, the love that promotes and protects life before God works for integrity, justice, and truth telling. It asks us to care for the relationships, things, and words that enable every person to have the life that God intends for him or her. It calls us to practice a spirit of generosity, as defined finally by Christ's self-giving love. It requires us to practice disciplines of love that reshape our inner core, our fundamental identity, so that we come to resemble Christ more fully.

This way of life must begin in the church. The church is called to be the salt of the earth and the light of the world. By the character of its own life, it is to show the world what God has also created the world to be.[16] The church rightly undertakes this responsibility only in a spirit of repentance, for it represents the way of Christ not by its own achievements, which are always ambiguous and infected with sin, but only by its confession of Christ, in whom alone this way of life is fulfilled. The church must continually examine itself in light of the commandments and confess its failures. At the same time, it must allow the commandments to mark out its way of life, for Christ has imprinted them on us in our baptism. As a church, we must find practices and disciplines of the commandments that strengthen our life together and allow us to face the world with a vision of the new heaven and the new earth.

Overcoming Anonymity

The sixth commandment raises questions about some of the most troubling issues in American society today—war, abortion, capital punishment, and domestic violence. As important as they are, they lie at the boundaries of the commandment, not at its heart. When broadened, applied to the inner life, and reversed, "Do not kill" does not focus on any act in particular but asks us to respect human life in general. Respect for life is, however, a complex phenomenon, especially in American society today.

Modern mass societies are incredibly effective at providing for the physical sustenance of their members; Americans, for example, live longer and healthier lives than ever before. But we are becoming less sensitive to each other in public life, less respectful. And although American society provides for a great deal of personal freedom, self-interest comes at the price of loneliness and isolation. A world of competing egos functions well for economic and even political ends, that is, for the free market and the free society. But such a world also leaves people feeling battered and bruised.

What does respect for life mean in that kind of world? Just a hundred years ago, Americans still lived in a world in which death was always near—and not just because of war. Even in the best of times, physical life was all too fragile. Too many babies died at birth or soon after. Just giving birth could threaten the life of the mother. A flu epidemic could suddenly take thousands of lives. Elderly people too often contracted pneumonia and died. There were no miracle drugs, no open-heart surgeries. Many cancers were inoperable. People with severe illnesses or injuries could be bedridden for days, even years, until they died what today we would call a premature death.

In such a world, every baby that survived birth represented a momentary victory of life over death; so too every child that made it to adolescence and then adulthood. Life could never be taken for granted. I was reminded of these realities a number of years ago when I hiked through Cumberland Gap National Park, near the spot where Virginia, Kentucky, and Tennessee meet. Daniel Boone and eventually two to three hundred thousand pioneers traveled through this area to get to the other side of the Appalachians. Most continued westward, but a few settled in the folds between the mountain ridges. Some even found small patches of arable land on nearby hilltops or sunny slopes. I stumbled upon just such a spot on a beautiful spring morning.

The trees and their first leaves, still wrinkled and wet like a newborn baby's skin, sparkled in the sunshine. The air was fresh and cool. I walked out of the forest into a clearing, where I found the remains of an old homestead. A rutted, dirt road still showed the way to and from the valley bottom, where the nearest homes and settlements lay. Up here on the isolated, windswept hillside, all was quiet. I tried to imagine what life must have been like a hundred years ago. The fields were small, perhaps just enough to support one family. The long ride up and down the bumpy road made it difficult if not impossible to get to school. A lovely and secluded retreat today, it was isolated back then.

Nearby a low, white picket fence marked out a square enclosure. I walked over, swung open the gate, and walked into the family graveyard. Fifteen or twenty tombstones stood on the site, most of them belonging to children. I was stunned as I read the dates. Several had died within their first hours and days; others were young children who must have played nearby in the high grass on a spring day like today's before disease or accident struck them down. Those who had died at a ripe old age were the exception in this place. Death had never been far away; the same fields in which this family had tried to raise its food had become the bed in which its members would find their final rest.

A hundred years later, what impresses us about the world is not how close death is, but how many living beings surround us. The old cemetery in Cumberland Gap National Park still offers us a free zone for meditation and reflection, but the busy world of human interests and intentions has filled the valley below and is slowly moving up the hillside. Today three times more people visit the national park *in just one year* than traveled through the gap from 1775–1810 to a new life on the frontier.[17]

Only a little over a hundred years ago, historian Frederick Jackson Turner was proclaiming the end of the frontier. No wild and wonderful places untouched by human (especially European) hands remained in America, he observed, and he wondered what the end of the frontier would mean for the national psyche. Up to that point, American identity had been profoundly shaped by the push westward into new, remote lands, with the space they offered for new ventures. The frontier had offered a safety valve, a place of escape and new beginnings. When Daniel Boone found Kentucky too crowded, he moved to Missouri!

In our time, a new threshold is being crossed. Not only is the frontier gone, but nearly every tract of land is actively used for one human purpose or another, whether commercial, retail, residential, agricultural, or recreational. I recently read that the state of New Jersey is rapidly reaching the point of being fully developed. A recent *National Geographic* magazine made a similar point about the country as a whole. The reader was invited to study a photographic image of the United States, taken from a space satellite at night. The image showed dots of light from major urban areas. One color represented urban/suburban borders ten years ago; another, their subsequent expansion. Almost everything east of the Mississippi was lit up! An accompanying article noted that America's cities have doubled in population over a period (1950–1990) in which they have quintupled in land mass. The suburbs keep stretching farther and farther into the countryside. The countryside itself is being settled more densely. The lines between urban, suburban, and exurban are becoming hazier.[18]

I love to camp, and the United States still offers large, protected areas in which I can imagine that I am getting away from it all. But even in such places, the crowds are growing. Foot trails through the Rockies can get as busy as city streets; in some areas, backpackers have to have permits, in an effort to control numbers and therefore to limit damage to the natural environment. But to me the most telling change since my childhood is in the skies. Several years ago, as I camped high in the Rockies, night fell, and the world grew silent. I could hear no human voice, automobile, television, or telephone—nothing of the human presence. Suddenly I started. I noticed a distant rumble, then another. For the next three hours, I heard one jet engine after another, carrying the day's last passengers—and the overnight, never-ending delivery services of UPS and Federal Express.

We are no longer the lonely pioneers on a remote hillside near Cumberland Gap, but the busy beavers whose appetite for the natural world is insatiable, with all the wreckage that comes in its wake. We try to get away from it all but cannot. And the human presence is increasingly impersonal, even threatening. It means crowded highways and noisy streets, polluted air and environmental degradation; more business for the economy, but also less pleasure in each other's presence. We cannot avoid each other, yet we are strangers; we call each other by first name but no longer mean anything personal by it.

The stranger has always represented both promise and threat. But to the people on the old farmstead near Cumberland Gap, the occasional stranger who wandered by also represented something more. Whether as friend or foe, he or she connected them to a larger world that still lay far away. Now that larger world presses in upon us. The stranger, like each of us, is merely one of billions of people on this earth—a mere breath, hardly of significance. The baby that survives to adulthood is no longer a miraculous victory of life over death but, rather, just one more body amidst a teeming mass of humanity that threatens to overwhelm us.

Mass society creates anonymity, and anonymity gives us considerable personal freedom. We don't have people looking over our shoulder all the time. We can pick and choose from a wide variety of cultural, educational, and entertainment offerings. We live where we like, dropping in and out of a host of voluntary associations, and developing the networks that we choose for business or personal purposes. Few of us would really thrive on the old farmstead; it is a wonderful respite from a busy, crowded world, but not a viable home.

But anonymous society also exacts a toll. Others easily become objects that impede our way. We are constantly bumping up against persons in the public square whom we do not know and whom we have no interest in ever knowing. We are all too busy pursuing our personal interests and just want others to stay out of our way. When they don't, our blood pressure rises. Someday, cultural historians, looking back on our time, will identify "road rage" as one of its symbolic markers. The automobile promises the personal freedom and flexibility that Americans prize. But we have to share the road with others who prize their personal freedom and flexibility too. The result is mounting frustration and anger. People become aggressive—and their aggression inevitably breeds more aggression. Someone cuts us off in traffic, and we curse them, knowing that we will never see each other again. What has happened to a society in which people regularly stretch red lights? Or where pedestrians cannot get across the street because no driver will stop? Or where no one obeys speed limits because the attitude is, "You leave me alone, and I'll leave you alone"?

Leaving each other alone is precisely what is so impossible in a mass society. We compete for the road, and because we don't really want to deal with others as individuals—with their quirks and weaknesses—we deal with our anger by stereotyping them. The person who has just cut us off becomes a blankety-blank feminist or redneck, Democrat or Republican, black or white—or some other, less honorable category. We make wild assumptions about their politics or home life, in a desperate effort to restore a sense of control to our lives. We don't really want to know the stranger personally, but we do want to believe that we know enough about them to put them in their place or get them out of our way or otherwise use them for our own purposes.

More generally, mass society teaches us to think of each other as mere material that can be studied, organized, and manipulated for one end or another.[19] We rightfully protest against police profiling but ignore the widespread practice of "economic profiling." Marketers can determine my salary and buying habits, and then direct their advertising to me, knowing that a certain percentage of persons in my category will respond positively. Loan officers can quickly assess my credit history. The Internal Revenue Service can feed my income tax information into a computer and generate a probability that I have cheated.

This ability to study, organize, and manipulate human life reaches its height in new reproductive technologies. Humans increasingly have the power to create life on their own terms. In vitro fertilization provides for the creation of human embryos outside the womb, with the possibility of implanting or destroying them. Scientists are learning to alter creatures' genetic makeup, as well as to clone them. Parents will soon be able to choose character traits or physical features for their children. Philosophers and theologians are increasingly perplexed about what it means to be human in a world in which the human is a work still in progress, but now seemingly under human rather than divine hands.

In our own way, in our own circumstances, we humans of the new millennium experience the profound contradictions that humans have always experienced about themselves. Life is at once infinitely valuable and incredibly cheap. We are able to save preterm babies at earlier and earlier stages, yet abortion is widely practiced. We take extraordinary measures to keep elderly, dying people on life support—in the midst of physician-assisted suicide and a "right to die" movement. We demand that every human be invested with unalienable rights to life, liberty, and the pursuit of happiness, yet depression is so widespread that Prozac is a household word.

We talk about a global society. What happens in one place or another on Mother Earth affects us all. Thanks to these global interconnections, we eat fresh fruits and vegetables all year round. But new diseases can be transmitted just as quickly from one country to another. Problems of global warming and environmental degradation, and also of terrorism and economic development, require new forms of international cooperation. In a broad, theoretical way, we are increasingly aware of how interdependent humans are and how much we need each other to solve the complex problems of our time.

Yet, in the smaller corners of our lives, we also have the sense that we are expendable, that no one really needs us. We too often live with the nagging feeling that we are just disposable human material, of which the world has too much already. Americans speak incessantly of the breakdown of community. Loneliness afflicts us, and we wonder if we fit and where we fit in a world that has become too big and complicated for us to manage anymore.

The twentieth century created antibiotics. It also created Auschwitz. The century that made it possible for us to communicate easily and efficiently with people thousands of miles away is also the century that made it possible for us to get along just fine without ever getting to know our next-door neighbors. As modern people, we have been taught that every individual is infinitely precious. Yet we are weary of the human presence, for it is a mostly nameless sea of humanity. We must negotiate our way through it, but we will never get to know it as distinct individual human beings.

To obey the sixth commandment under these circumstances is to do the work of remembering who humans really are in the eyes of God. It is to reclaim our baptismal identity, knowing that it points to the true identity of every human being before God. The interconnections between us are not just sociological, biological, economic, or political. More profoundly, they are spiritual. To respect life is to discover a mysterious God-given connection between us all, perhaps also between humans and the rest of the creation.

In the words of Fyodor Dostoyevsky, the great Russian novelist, who struggled with similar questions about mass society:

> Love all God's creation, the whole of it and every grain of sand. Love every leaf, every ray of God's light! Love the animals, love the plants, love everything. If you love everything, you will perceive the divine mystery in things. And once you have perceived it, you

> will begin to comprehend it ceaselessly more and more every day. And you will at last come to love the whole world with an abiding, universal love. . . .
>
> Love man even in his sin, for that already bears the semblance of divine love and is the highest love on earth.[20]

In traditional Christian explications of the sixth commandment, the deepest expression of this divinely crafted interconnection between humans has been the love of enemies that Christ himself commended and practiced:

> You have heard that it was said, "You shall love your neighbor and hate your enemy." But I say to you, Love your enemies and pray for those who persecute you, so that you may be children of your Father in heaven; for he makes his sun rise on the evil and on the good, and sends rain on the righteous and on the unrighteous. For if you love those who love you, what reward do you have? Do not even the tax collectors do the same? (Matt. 5:43–46)

Nothing is more difficult and nothing takes greater practice and discipline than the work of reconciliation. Reconciliation is difficult enough within a nation or a church or even a family. But how in the world does the soldier who killed the enemy soldier make peace with the enemy's wife or children? How does the citizen on whose behalf the soldier killed make peace with the enemy soldier who would have to tried kill him, had he stood in the way? And how does reconciliation between nations take place, when they are not simply collections of individuals, but complex social organizations in which any sense of personal responsibility is quickly mitigated by feelings of utter powerlessness? Whatever else it means, reconciliation in such a world will be a process that never ends this side of the grave.[21]

Today the challenge of reconciliation is greater than ever. Technological advances in weaponry, as well as the growth of human populations, magnify the crimes that peoples and nations are capable of committing against each other. The overwhelming military and economic dominance of the United States is fueling new resentments in other parts of the globe. The Cold War has ended, but new, regional conflicts have emerged. Nations and fanatical groups continue to train killers, in large part by teaching them to deny the enemy's humanity.

In the new world of war, powerful nations are able to reduce the enemy to nothing more than a blip on a computer screen; soldiers launch pinpoint accurate attacks, never seeing the faces of their victims until they are dead—and given the power of our weaponry, we may so annihilate them that no faces are left at all, but only a few body parts that are swept together and deposited in black bags.

In response to the overwhelming power of the nation-state, new forms of terrorism have emerged, successfully exploiting the anonymity of modern, mass societies (especially in the democratic, pluralistic West) for their own wicked purposes. As suicide bombers (and states' punitive responses) have already taught us, even civilians will be fair game, because they too will be regarded as nothing more than symbolic representatives of the unrighteous cause of the other side.

But, as I have suggested, there is an even greater danger to human life today than war. In mass, anonymous society, we have difficulty seeing the humanity not only of the enemy far away but also of the neighbor next door. We objectify, classify, and categorize the people whom we encounter in everyday life, all in the name of guaranteeing that they will not get too much in our way. We learn to treat each other as programmable, manageable beings that can give us what we want and be discarded when we no longer find them useful. We put everyone into his or her place, only to doubt that we ourselves really have a place, a home, on this earth.

In this kind of world, we desperately need practices and disciplines of respecting life that will train us to resist this pervasive anonymity. We will have to work hard at resisting our tendency to treat others as mere statistics or material. Only with great effort will we come to a greater awareness that a failure to see the image of God in others ultimately "kills" them—and us. Whenever we break through the anonymity of daily life, whenever we remember to treat another as a child of God and not simply as a potential help or impediment to our own agenda, we will be walking in the way of the sixth commandment and therefore in the way of Jesus' self-giving love.

We will regularly fail at this task. The conditions of modern, mass society place us in daily contact with far more people than we can ever get to know as human persons; life in modern society will never run out of anonymity. We can make a beginning, however, by learning to recognize places of weakness in our lives and others'—for that weakness exposes us as vulnerable, fragile human flesh that desperately needs care and respect. Weakness is ultimately what makes us human—the fact of our utter dependence on powers and forces outside our own control that give us basic nourishment, human friendship, and spiritual sustenance. We are not self-created; from the very beginning, each of us has *received* life. Whenever we remember our baptism, we remember the God who spoke an identity into our nameless, anonymous life. Whenever we learn to speak to others as beloved ones of God, we name them for who they really are in the eyes of God.

The sixth commandment directs us to practices and disciplines of reaching out to others as beings who, like us, are ultimately weak and powerless. Where we see others suffer, we will strive not to pass by on the other side of the road, but to stop and reach out, acknowledging them as human flesh in all its beauty and vulnerability. When we see walls and barriers that nations throw up against each other out of mutual fear, we will strive to cultivate personal friendships with people on the other side. Whatever depersonalizes others, we will resist; conversely, whenever we take the time to let the other truly be a person in our sight, we will be living out the sixth commandment.[22]

Making time for others; showing hospitality to the stranger, whether he or she lives next door or far away; remembering that others are weak, vulnerable flesh like us—these practices and disciplines will keep us occupied for a lifetime. They will begin in our families—in the ways we learn to live together with our differences, and in the ways we invite others from outside to share in the family's life. The family can teach us to pay attention to each other and to respect each other's places of weakness and injury, vulnerability and disability.

But if our true family and our true brothers and sisters are in the church, then the church in particular has the responsibility to embody the sixth commandment in its way of life. Attention to baptismal identity will teach us to face each other in Christian love so that we might see each other as the wondrous treasures that God created us to be. We will learn to be both patients and nurses in that grand hospital for sinners that is the church.[23]

Sacraments That Make Relationship Possible

The parents stand at the font with the baby, but first the minister must turn to the congregation and ask a question:

> Do you, as members of the church of Jesus Christ,
> promise to guide and nurture Hannah Ruth
> by word and deed,

with love and prayer,
encouraging her to know and follow Christ
and to be a faithful member of his church?[24]

Whenever a baby is baptized, a congregation pledges not to leave her alone in anonymity, but to know her and call her by name. That child is now part of the church family, and we promise to be her fathers and mothers, brothers and sisters. Congregations, of course, regularly fail in this task, just as each of us individually succumbs to forces of anonymity again and again. The congregation may be large enough that we never really get to know most of the children. Or the baby may be baptized, and the parents never darken the door of the church building again. Thoughtful church members sometimes wonder whether they can take these vows with integrity.

But these vows implicitly commit us not only to the children in our midst. Whether we ever see that newly baptized baby again or not, her baptism ought to remind us of our responsibility to care for every member of the congregation. Will we remember to look others in the face and see their humanity? Will we bear each other's burdens and seek reconciliation in the face of our disagreements? Will we attend church primarily in order to fulfill personal needs or, instead, for the sake of growing in Christian faith and therefore in self-giving love?

Calvin once noted that if God has generally bound humans together one to another, how much more should Christians be concerned to honor and respect their brothers and sisters in the faith.[25] By their baptism, they belong to Christ. They have become members of one body. In the church of all places, we are called to break down walls of anonymity and to know each other in our God-given connection. Calvin believed that the Lord's Supper would strengthen us in these commitments to each other:

> We shall very much benefit from the Sacrament if this thought is impressed and engraved on our minds: that none of the brethren can be injured, despised, rejected, abused, or in any way offended by us, without at the same time, injuring, despising, and abusing Christ by the wrongs we do . . . that we cannot love God without loving him in the brethren; that we ought to take the same care of our brethren's bodies as we take of our own . . . [and that] we ought not to allow a brother to be afflicted by any evil, without being touched by compassion for him.[26]

The Lord's Supper is intimately related to the sixth commandment. It is a sacrament of life, a receiving of God's self-giving love in Christ, so that we in turn might learn to give of ourselves to God and our brothers and sisters, and thus respect and preserve life. But the training that takes place in the church is never for the sake of the church alone. The Lord's Supper and the sixth commandment also point us to the world. They direct us to those who are our enemies. The church's practices and disciplines prepare us for a coming kingdom, where "they shall beat their swords into plowshares, and their spears into pruning hooks; nation shall not lift up sword against nation, neither shall they learn war any more" (Micah 4:3).

The Supper, the commandments, and the corresponding practices and disciplines of faith remind us that baptism is never just for people who would rather turn inward, away from the intrusive eyes of the world, but, rather, takes place before the world. When the baptismal ceremony is over, we leave the font and the sanctuary and carry our baptismal identity into the world. If we truly understand what baptism is all about, it is never a private but always a public event. Together, father and mother, minister, and congregation declare to the world, "Look at this little one. See the marks of Christ on her. And look at us too. We stand with her." Every baptism involves an act of personal and corporate confession of faith, of looking the world in the face and saying, "We believe in this God, and we believe that we belong in life and in death to him—and you do too."

After many years, a woman returns to the sanctuary in which her father and mother once held her as a baby before a minister and a congregation. But now she stands by herself at the font, and it is no longer a Sunday morning but a weekday afternoon. The room is dark and empty. She closes her eyes and pictures a sweet, idyllic scene. She wonders whether everything wasn't better in her childhood. Family, church, and childhood gave her a home, a free space. Now life has become a lot more complicated. There are tensions at work, demands at home from spouse and children. She doesn't understand why she gets along with some people and not with others, or how she has come to have enemies. Words such as *estrangement* and *alienation*, which meant nothing to her in her childhood, have become all too tragically clear.

But if she has been sustained by practices and disciplines of baptismal identity, she will not stay there for long. She will know that her place is not in an idyllic past but in the messy, present-day world, where God is at work in people's weakness and powerlessness. She can now face the world; she can bear it, because she knows that whatever her failures, she can commend the stranger and even the enemy to God, in whose eyes no one is finally faceless or nameless.

Chapter Six

Eucharist

Satisfy us in the morning with your steadfast love, so that we may rejoice and be glad all our days.

Ps. 90:14

Few middle-class Americans have ever gone to bed hungry or thirsty. My parents threatened a couple of times when I had misbehaved as a child to send me to my room without supper, but they never did. In my adult life, a refrigerator, a restaurant, or a grocery store has never been far away.

But one time in my life I was so thirsty that I was scared—scared that I might die of dehydration. I was a young man, out of college and between jobs. I had taken a month to hike and backpack in Colorado, the first time that I had gone off into the wilderness by myself. Any experienced hiker knows that you shouldn't hike by yourself—too many things can go wrong. But I was staying on established trails and was returning every three or four days to civilization in order to replenish my supplies. Young men do crazier things than that. I was sure that I would be safe.

The weather had turned hot, but the trail ran by a nice stream. I made camp for the night and fixed my dinner. As I studied the map, I decided that the next day I would climb a pass to the other side of the range. When I left in the morning, I didn't think to fill my canteen. It was another hot, sunny day, and the exertion of climbing the steep slope wore me out. By mid-morning I was ready for a break, and then I discovered that I had no water. No worry. I knew that wherever you walk in the Rocky Mountains, you can count on coming across tumbling streams. The land is dry, but the winter snowpack is always sufficient to keep streams running throughout the summer. Lower elevations may dry out, but if you keep hiking toward timberline, you will eventually find water.

I had no such luck. The mountains were not as high as I had expected; the elevations never rose above timberline, and as I climbed, the terrain only got drier. The few streams that would have run in the spring were now long dry. By mid-afternoon, my clothes were soaked with perspiration, but I had still come across no water. I was getting thirsty, really thirsty. I had several choices. I could return down the mountainside to where I had made my camp the day before, but then I would lose two days travel time and would not have enough food to hike out. I could keep going, but I could not be sure that I would come across water. I was at the top of the pass, and the brilliant sunshine still beat down upon me. I was dehydrated and weak, and my maps did not indicate any place that I could find a spring or stream.

I soon found that I couldn't think clearly, and my options seemed more and more limited. I didn't have the energy to return to my previous camp. What should I do? Make camp here, go to bed thirsty, and hope that I would have better luck tomorrow? Try hiking down to a highway and hitching a ride into town? But late afternoon was already turning into evening. I didn't have time to hike out. A growing sense of panic gripped me. I began to run almost wildly down the mountain path. Frustrated and afraid, I finally flung myself to the ground, cursing myself for my stupidity. There, in the cool shade of the forest, I closed my eyes and waited, I'm not sure for what.

Nothing seemed to move, but after a few minutes, I noticed a humming sound. Bees? I opened my eyes and looked up. Yes, there were bees nearby. What were bees doing up here on a mountain pass on a hot summer afternoon? I stood up and walked over a few feet to a secluded spot where ten or twenty bees had nestled on the ground. As I looked more closely, I discovered that they were actually hovering on the surface of a tiny pool of water. There in the cool shade, they had found respite. They were not interested in me; like me, they were just trying to escape the heat. I took out a metal cup, carefully filled it with water, and quivered with joy as I slowly drank to my heart's content.

Give Us Our Daily Bread

Years later, I heard of a similar experience from a young man visiting his family in Pittsburgh. In a search for identity, he had become Orthodox several years earlier and had moved to Russia. He had little money; only his parents' generosity made it possible for him to return home every summer. He told me of the deprivations that Russians had faced in the first years after the demise of the Communist government and the rise of Boris Yeltsin. Food became scarce; the markets that had once been filled with produce from the countryside were empty as farmers and consumers hesitatingly felt their way into a market economy. For a time, everyone in the cities was hungry. But one day my friend found an egg for sale, one lonely, lovely egg. As he left the market, he skipped down the streets of Moscow, the egg perched perilously in his hand. "An egg, an egg, I have an egg," he sang to himself.

A tiny pool of water on a hot summer day. A solitary egg, after months of stale potatoes. Simple joys, as profound nevertheless as the joy of a shepherd who has located a lost sheep, or a woman who has just found a lost coin. Hunger and thirst expose our weakness and powerlessness. They remind us of our vulnerability and human frailty. We are mere flesh and blood, subject to injury and disease. Famine and drought are never far away. But we Americans, who have so much, easily forget how precious food and drink really are.

Hunger and thirst are never simply physical phenomena; they teach us spiritual truths. Body and soul are intricately interconnected. The cool water that I poured down my parched throat on that dry mountain pass was more refreshing than the finest wine that I have ever tasted. With every swallow, I could feel that water coursing like joy through my body. My despair and confusion quickly dissipated; I paused again in wonder at the trees and earth and blue sky that surrounded me on a beautiful summer day.

In the same way, the egg that once danced in my friend's fingers represented more than physical nutrition; it caused hope to stir in his heart again. He knew that he was privileged to participate in the beginnings of a new political era fraught with danger but also new freedoms. The physical was giving birth to the spiritual; food and drink became reminders of larger historical realities.

We should not be surprised that the first temptation of Jesus in the wilderness had to do with food. After forty days of fasting, Jesus was famished. He had plumbed the human condition and knew just how hungry and thirsty men and women can become. Satan told him to satisfy his hunger by turning rock into bread. Like the serpent speaking to Adam and Eve, the devil reminded Jesus that God would not want to deprive him of good food and healthy living.

Full stomachs keep us quiet. They reassure us that life is good, that we can hold body and soul together one more day. Conversely, hunger and thirst make us anxious. They tempt us to believe that life is spinning out of control, that God is not reliable, and that we have to live by domination and self-assertion rather than by trust and thanksgiving.

But hunger and thirst can also teach us that humans ultimately live in a state of dependence. If we understand them rightly, we have to confess that we receive life as God's gift. Even the energies that we expend in taking care of ourselves and our basic needs are finally sustained by powers and forces from beyond ourselves. Every day of our lives, we are dependent on food and drink to keep us alive. We never eat and drink once and for all; we have to eat and drink again and again, and so we continually pray, "Give us this day, our *daily* bread."

So too we are dependent on God's grace for our basic identity. We can never simply choose to be whoever we want. Nor will we ever know ourselves well enough to say, "I finally have it all together. I have no need of God or others." Dependence on daily bread symbolizes our dependence on God for our life's meaning and purpose. Our baptismal identity, like our physical energies, must be renewed every day. We need daily sustenance in the life to which Christ has called us. For that reason, "one does not live by bread alone, but by every word that comes from the mouth of God" (Matt. 4:4).

This daily sustenance comes to Christians in Word, sacrament, and patterns and rhythms of life together. God feeds us again and again. God continually renews our capacity to receive Christ's self-giving love and, then, to offer our very selves to God and others. "Give us this day, our daily bread" is never just a call for physical nourishment, but is also a plea for the bread of heaven that is life in the risen Lord.[1]

In the end, Jesus himself must feed us and quench our thirst. He declares, "I am the bread of life. Whoever comes to me will never be hungry, and whoever believes in me will never be thirsty" (John 6:35), for "the water that I will give them will become in them a spring of water gushing up to eternal life" (John 4:14).[2] Christians have found this spiritual food and drink whenever they have celebrated the Eucharist. Baptism first marks us in our new identity in Christ, while the Eucharist gives us strength to persist in our baptismal identity, even in the midst of trial and temptation. Baptism sends us into the world, and the Eucharist offers us food and drink for the journey. Baptism tells us who we really are, and the Eucharist deepens and confirms our identity. Font leads to table. The helpless baby we place in God's hands will surely receive the basic nutrition that she needs to live out her baptism.

Christ's Very Life

We can go for a while without food; the greatest monks claimed that they could go as long as Jesus' forty days. We can go for a while without drink, but scientists tell us that even under the most favorable of conditions, we will live only for a week or ten days without water. Even if we gorge our bodies with food and drink and try to hoard them in our cells, we soon grow hungry and thirsty again. Like the manna in the wilderness that was good only for the day, so too the food and drink that we enjoy today mostly lasts us only until the morrow. We do not like the sensation of an empty stomach or a dry mouth. We do not like to grow weak and listless. We like it so little that most of us eat three good meals a day and drink numerous cups of coffee, tea, juices, soft drinks, and water throughout the day. We don't do well without our daily bread.

Our lives depend on calories that are not our own. We live off of plants and animals. Other beings give up their life so that we can have food, nutrition, and life. Humans have often developed rituals of giving thanks for the plant and animal life that they take in order to sustain themselves. They may speak of "sacrificing" other forms of life and may even ask forgiveness for their actions. This concern to respect not only human life but also other forms of life is also present in Judaism and Christianity. Moses instructed the people of Israel not to eat animal flesh with the blood still in it. The blood represented the animal's life force and had to be treated with special respect (see Lev. 17:10–14). Christians believed that these regulations had been annulled in Christ (though at the Jerusalem Council, the Jewish Christians still asked the Gentiles to abstain from blood [Acts 15:20]). But like Jews they believed that they owed God thanks for all his sustaining gifts. Their gratitude acknowledged their dependence on life sources from beyond themselves.

Martin Luther's table instructions illustrate the kind of thanksgiving and dependence that belong to the Christian life. When the members of the household gathered at the table, they were reverently to fold their hands and lift up the words of the psalmist:

> The eyes of all wait upon you, O Lord,
>   and you give them good in their due season.
> You open wide your hand,
>   and satisfy the needs of every living thing.
>
> Ps. 145:15–16

At the end of the meal, they were to pray again, now giving thanks to God for having sustained them in their weakness and powerlessness: "O give thanks to the LORD, for he is good; for his steadfast love endures forever" (Ps. 106:1).[3]

Just as we live off physical calories that are not our own, we live off "spiritual calories" that are not our own. When we eat and drink physically, we take other forms of life into ourselves. We ingest them, and they pass into us and become part of us. So too, at the Lord's Supper we testify that Christ's life has passed into our own. Many Christian theologians have not hesitated to speak of a union with the living Lord that is represented or effected through the Supper. While they have debated the mechanics and means of this union, they have not doubted that it is as real and intimate as the union of physical food and drink with our very cells.[4]

Some Christians have believed that they were ingesting the literal body and blood of Jesus as they partook of the eucharistic bread and wine. Others have insisted that the bread and wine are merely symbolic of a union that has already taken place by the Holy Spirit through faith. Still others have spoken of Christ's spiritual power, which passes into us when we eat the eucharistic meal and trust in the promises that accompany it.

Whatever else may be at stake in these theological debates, all three ways of thinking about Eucharist point to our creaturely dependence on God. Whatever life in Christ is all about, we cannot effect it out of our own resources. We do not have within ourselves the wisdom and courage to live according to Christ's self-giving love; we receive it as a possibility from beyond ourselves. God alone offers us this way of life, and he offers it to us by offering his very self to us.

Scripture tells us that at the Last Supper,

> [Jesus] took a loaf of bread, and when he had given thanks, he broke it and said, "Take, eat; this is my body." In the same way, he took a cup, and after giving thanks, he gave it to them, saying, "Drink from it all of you; for this is my blood of the covenant, which is poured out for many for the forgiveness of sins. . . . As often as you eat this bread and drink this cup, you proclaim the Lord's death until he comes." (Matt. 26:26–28 and 1 Cor. 11:24–26, conflated)

In the Supper, Christ, the Son of God incarnate, feeds us his very life, energy, and calories. He allows us to take himself into us. This thought so moved John Calvin that he wrote, "Although he is in heaven and we are on earth, we are nevertheless flesh of his flesh and bone of his bone."[5] "Christ pours his life into us, as if it penetrated our bones and marrow."[6] The believer is "now quickened by [Christ's] immortal flesh, and in a sense partakes of his immortality."[7] The Eucharist reminds us that we truly live by possibilities that are not our own.

As I write these words, I think of all the wondrous things that I have been privileged to experience over my lifetime: people who reached out to me in my times of weakness and powerlessness, as when I traveled overseas and depended on others' good graces—sometimes for food and drink and shelter, and always for friendship and encouragement; times that I sat with German friends in beautiful backyard gardens on cool spring evenings, and we ate together and chatted and reveled in each other's company; teachers and mentors, students and colleagues, Christian brothers and sisters, and so many others who helped to make my life what it is.

I remember moments of joyful praise in church, as though I were joining heavenly choirs; life in family—the sacrifices that my parents made for me, and the unexpected joys that marriage and children have brought; hikes in the mountains of Colorado and British Columbia and elsewhere, and stunning landscapes, awesome sunsets, and star-studded, nighttime skies; and strangers who offered me a helping hand when I was lost or afraid and could not find my way home.

I am aware of how fragile these experiences have been. How some friendships that I once thought so deep gradually petered out. How family life has brought disappointments, as well as joys. How natural moments of beauty have always snuck up on me and then disappeared as soon as I tried to hold on to them. How I have had to recognize my own limits physically, intellectually, and spiritually. How each of us lives in the valley of the shadow of death.

When I turned forty-nine and had lived more years than my father, I began to tell myself that each day was truly God's gracious gift—more than I could ever have expected to experience. Perhaps you, like I, also look back over your life and see how in good times and bad you were threatened by powers and forces that you could not understand, but were nevertheless sustained by other powers and forces equally mysterious. We have all experienced moments of sheer terror and utter joy, and perhaps the quiet confidence that God somehow was working in both cases to make us more trusting in him.

God has given us of the divine life as God has touched us with joyful and privileged moments. God has become weak and powerless in Christ, that we might know God's sustaining presence in our own weakness and powerlessness. God has allowed us to face the world with all its hopes and fears. There are times that you and I have nothing more to offer to God than the simple words, "Thanks. Thanks be to God." Nothing more, and nothing less.

Exodus, Eschatology, and Eucharist

At that Last Supper, Jesus took bread and gave thanks. Ever since, his followers too have taken bread and given thanks. They have received Christ's self-giving love, and they have responded by giving themselves to God and others in gratitude. This giving of thanks is itself a giving of the self, a way of confirming the identity that we have received in Jesus Christ. When we give thanks, we turn outward and away from ourselves. We acknowledge our dependence on God and on the world that God has given us.

Gratitude characterized every meal that Jesus shared, whether with tax collectors and sinners, or with weak-willed disciples. Gratitude will also characterize the heavenly banquet in which our baptismal identity will come to complete fulfillment. Hungry and thirsty people know that food and drink come to them as wondrous gifts of God, symbols of a kingdom in which "death will be no more; mourning and crying and pain will be no more" (Rev. 21:4).

The Gospel of John tells of such a meal on a mountain by the Sea of Galilee. This story, like other Gospel accounts of a feeding of four or five thousand, echoes with Old Testament imagery. John tells us that the miracle took place at the time of the Passover (John 6:4). Philip's question, "Where are we to buy bread for these people to eat?" recalls Moses' in the wilderness, "Where am I to get meat to give to all this people?" (Num. 11:13). Even closer is the parallel to the Old Testament prophet Elisha, who tells his servant to feed a hundred people with twenty loaves of bread (2 Kings 4:42–44). Like Philip, the servant protests that the loaves will not suffice, and both stories end with food left over. The bread that Jesus breaks reminds us of God's miraculous provision for the people of Israel during the exodus and the forty years in the wilderness.

The story not only looks back to the exodus but also ahead to the end of time. The mountain on which the crowd gathers reminds us of the mountain on which God has promised to "make for all peoples a feast of rich food" (Isa. 25:6). All humanity will someday gather on that mountain, in praise and thanksgiving to God (Isa. 66:20–23; Rev. 21:24–26). It is the mountain of the New Jerusalem, the symbol of God's new heaven and new earth.

What connects the salvation that has already come (exodus) and God's coming kingdom (eschatology) is Eucharist. Note John's eucharistic-like language: "Jesus took the loaves, and when he had given thanks, he distributed them to those who were seated; so also the fish, as much as they wanted" (John 6:11). The five loaves and two fish that a mere lad in the crowd had supplied proved to be more than enough for five thousand men, just as the eucharistic elements, though barely enough to give each of us a taste, feed us all. Indeed, there is always more than enough: "From the fragments of the five barley loaves, left by those who had eaten, [the disciples] filled twelve baskets" (John 6:13).

When the Gospel of John later describes Jesus' Last Supper (chap. 13), it tells of a foot washing, but not of the institution of a eucharistic meal. Eucharist comes not at the end of Jesus' life but here, in the story of the feeding of the five thousand. To the misunderstanding crowd, the miracle is the multiplication of food. In response, Jesus tells them of "the bread of God . . . [that] comes down from heaven and gives life to the world" (John 6:33). The true miracle is that Jesus himself has become this bread of heaven. A little bit of food on a mountainside, like the bread and the cup at the Supper, miraculously conveys Jesus' very life and presence to those who believe in him.

Eucharist and Sabbath

In faithful eucharistic practice, Christians rehearse the way of life for which the commandments have marked us. The meal invites us into the Sabbath time of the fourth commandment. The bread and wine offer us a foretaste of a heavenly banquet at which we will someday sit. We are invited even now to *rest* in Christ's presence and in the presence of all who belong to him. We are asked to cast off every anxious, self-interested concern of this life, every hindrance to right relationship with God and others. Eucharist calls us to practice communion, life together as people who live for each other, to the glory of God.[8]

No eucharistic celebration in this world perfectly fulfills these divine promises. The bread and wine have no magical power to make us better, more spiritual people. We do not suddenly become super-Christians, nourished by supercalories from a divine source. We may not find anything inspiring or renewing about a particular celebration of the Lord's

Supper. The people who gather for Eucharist are still flawed humans, distracted by their cares and concerns, even resentful perhaps of something that the pastor or a fellow worshiper has said or done. We always gather as weak people—all too hungry and thirsty, if we are honest with ourselves.

What Eucharist gives us is not a product but a pathway, not a result but a road. Eucharist sets us on a course to deeper life in God and faithfulness to each other. We cannot yet reach our life destination, but we do see it from afar. We can know that God made us for intimate, trusting relationship. We can know that we have a future with God and others, despite the failures of the past. Eucharist calls us to practice and discipline a way of life. It offers us a Sabbath free zone in which we can remember again who we really are and therefore what we believe we are destined to become by virtue of our baptism.

Eucharist and Interdependence

The eucharistic meal invites us into the practices and disciplines of mutual submission that the fifth commandment sets forth. Someone hands us a piece of bread and says, "The body of Christ given for you." The same person or another hands us a cup and says, "The blood of Christ shed for you." What we receive reminds us that Christ submitted to our sinful human condition, bearing it all the way to the cross. What we receive also reminds us of the brother or sister in Christ who honors us by serving us the elements. The bread and the wine are neither theirs nor ours to keep; nevertheless, they and we now have the privilege of sharing the elements with each other. Eucharist tells us that we are members of one body, each with distinct gifts and abilities for the good of the whole.

In the Eucharist, someone serves us, and we may also be asked to serve the bread and the cup to another. The man or woman whom we might otherwise avoid on Sunday morning suddenly becomes the brother or sister in Christ, on our right or left. The elderly woman, the divorced man, and the teenager with the pierced nose become our fathers and mothers in the faith, and we become father and mother to them. It all seems so ridiculous, this eucharistic meal—people who have gathered for a multitude of reasons good and bad, people who have brought their boredom and hope, sorrow and love, to a simple wooden table, and who now pause, chew a piece of bread, and swallow a gulp of wine. We are a motley crew, and yet the eucharistic promises assert that we have been given each other for the work of life together, beginning with our baptism.

Eucharist does not cover up our sinful, flawed state. It does not magically remove the differences and disagreements, the irritations and infractions, that we inevitably experience in each other's presence. We are not asked to squeeze our eyes together and make everything blurry and pretend that the church and its members are suddenly a lovely, attractive body of believers. All that the Eucharist can do is set us on our feet and show us the way that God first marked out for us in our baptism. Eucharist is an invitation to learn practices and disciplines of interdependence, starting here with the bread and cup that we pass to each other.[9]

Eucharist and Life

The eucharistic meal invites us to respect life, in the spirit of the sixth commandment. Each member of the body must be concerned for the other members. In the words of the apostle Paul, "If one member suffers, all suffer together with it; if one member is honored, all rejoice together with it" (1 Cor. 12:26). Eucharist thus calls us to care about what is happening in each other's lives. The Christ who feeds us at this table also asks us to feed each other at the tables of daily life. The bread and wine that we eat together here must commit us to ensure that every person receives his or her daily bread in the world that we face.

Eucharist promotes and protects life by asking us to know and call each other by name: "*Hannah Ruth*, the body of Christ given for you," or "*Elizabeth Anne*, the blood of Christ shed for you." Even when we do not know the given name of the person on our right or left, we can surely say, "My brother, the body of Christ," or "My sister, the blood of Christ." If nothing else, we can hold them in our hearts, asking God to care for them as much as for others whom we know personally and care about.

Eating together calls us into living together. A child has a birthday, and the parents prepare a special birthday dinner, culminating in ice cream and cake. A couple has an anniversary, and they go out to eat at a fancy restaurant. A graduation, an achievement, or a promotion is celebrated, and people gather and eat something; they want to share table with each other. They want to be with each other and to enjoy each other's company. Eucharist too calls us to experience communion and therefore to break down every wall of hostility and anonymity.

We regularly fail. Too often we eat this meal like the fast food that we pick up at a drive-by counter. Rather than serving each other, we grab for ourselves. Rather than calling each other by name, we let the Lord's Supper be more anonymous than the fellowship time that follows worship. Although we sit in a pew surrounded by brothers and sisters in Christ, we choose to eat alone in our own little world. Eucharist can be celebrated with liturgical precision yet taken unfaithfully if it becomes little more than an ingrown moment of personal or communal self-absorption. Eucharist matters only to the degree that it exercises us together in faith and disciplines us together in the fruit of the Spirit. The grace of the Lord Jesus Christ must slowly but inexorably shape us into a people of gratitude.

As strange as it might seem, gratitude is not simply a spontaneous reaction to God's goodness. We must learn thankfulness again and again. We must come to see the Eucharist as a discipline that we *practice*. We must be reminded again and again that Jesus gives his life for the world, and that Jesus asks his followers to give thanks. Whatever self-giving love we learn, it never takes the place of the cross, where God empties himself for the world. But whenever we give thanks to God, we point in some small yet profound way to what God has done for the world. Our thanks will never take the place of God's love, but it can reflect it.

Losing Ourselves

Throughout these pages, I have spoken of spiritual practices and disciplines that help sustain us in our baptismal identity. These practices and disciplines cannot guarantee that we will grow in faith. They offer no automatic results. We can nevertheless trust that they are pathways along which the Holy Spirit regularly works. Whenever we do such things as keep Sabbath, submit to each other in love, and respect life, the Spirit opens us to its renewing power. It uses these practices and disciplines to shape the rhythms of our daily lives, personally and communally; it gives us the confidence that we are indeed growing in joy, gratitude, humility, gentleness, and peace (see Gal. 5:22).

Even at our best, we fall desperately short of living out our baptismal identity. Practices and disciplines that should be life-giving easily become distorted.[10] Keeping Sabbath (living in God's free zones) is reduced to legalistic posturing, or alternatively becomes little more than a day dedicated to personal leisure. Mutual submission for the sake of interdependence (honoring "father" and "mother") becomes a destructive pattern of what psychologists call codependence. Breaking through anonymity (respecting and promoting rather than diminishing life) becomes a matter of inappropriate intrusion into another's life, rather than life-giving relationship with that person.

Even when these practices and disciplines escape severe distortion, they are, as I have noted, remarkably fragile. In chapter 4, I reflected on family devotions and spoke of how the slightest change in schedule easily undercuts a discipline that my family and I have been practicing for nearly ten years. I would like to believe that Christian practices and disciplines are so vital that people cannot do without them. But my own experience belies that assumption.

Each new day presents us with new challenges. As soon as we awaken and open our eyes, we wonder: Will we stay grounded today in our baptismal identity? Will we remember who we really are? Will we live in the way of Christ, guided by the fruit of the Spirit? Or will we fall apart? Will self-interest or self-pity consume us, despite our best intentions to the contrary?

Christians know how desperately they need God's renewing Spirit every day. Scripture reminds us that "when you open your hand, [we] are filled with good things. When you hide your face, [we] are dismayed; when you take away [our] breath, [we] die and return to [our] dust" (Ps. 104:28–29). And Peter asked, "Lord, to whom can we go? You have the words of eternal life" (John 6:68).

Most of the time, life goes along as usual, and we feel confident that our faith is strong. We may have prayed that morning, may have read our Bible. We feel certain that for all our faults, we are nevertheless growing in faith. But then something unexpected happens that suddenly triggers a reaction of fear or anger. We panic, or experience self-doubt. The "something" may be a major event: the death of a loved one, a battle with illness, or a crushing disappointment over the job that we did not get or the relationship that ended. More often than not, the trigger is amazingly trivial; someone said a word that hit us the wrong way, or a person cut us off in traffic, or we just got tired of having to clean up after the kids or our spouse one more time.[11]

In colloquial English, we use the expression "I lost it." To lose it is to feel that our lives have suddenly fallen apart. We dissolve into tears, or "lose" our temper, or "lose" our composure. For a moment, we don't know anymore who we really are. Something inside of us snaps, and we feel as though we are no longer ourselves. What we have lost is not just "it," but ourselves.

I am generally an even-tempered, pleasant person. I am not easily ruffled, and I like to get along with others. But, like any person, I have my weak spots, my places of special sensitivity. As a young boy, I used to walk home from school, and one day a couple of dogs leapt off a porch, charged me, and bit me. The bites were not severe, but ever since I have been afraid of strange dogs. I now like to jog in a large, wooded park near my home. But dog owners regularly let their dogs off-leash, despite signs that clearly warn them against it. More than once I have had large dogs come running at me, bark at me, and even jump up on me, their owners nonchalantly walking along or perhaps calling out to me that their dogs are just being friendly. But something goes off inside of me. My heart beats faster; my blood pressure goes up. My body senses danger, and my first impulse is to stop and shake my fist and scream at the dog and its owner. I feel as though I am being violated, and what is worse is that the dog owner doesn't care. I count for less in her eyes than her dog.

More times than I would like to admit, I have not been able to repress my impulse to blow up. What has come to worry me over time is not my anger; I am convinced that my anger is justified, and I am also convinced that offending dog owners need to know that I am angry. What does worry me is that my anger is so explosive. It bursts out and is no more respectful of others than they have been of me. By the time I get back home, I feel shame, if not guilt. I then ask myself, What is wrong with me that I lose my cool? Why do I so easily lose myself?

For a good while, I prayed about my anger. For a while, I avoided the park altogether. Then I tried to be a good medieval monk, willing to submit patiently to whatever God sent my way. Sometimes I succeeded in holding my tongue; sometimes I stopped and asked people politely to leash their dog. Inevitably, however, I would lose my cool again after a few weeks. I have had to learn that I just don't know in advance how I will react when a dog comes at me.

During Lent, one of the psalms that regularly cycles through the morning prayer lectionary is Psalm 22. My kids and I chuckle whenever we read, "Dogs are all around me; a company of evildoers encircles me. . . . But you, O LORD, do not be far away! O my help, come quickly to my aid! Deliver . . . my life from the power of the dog!" (vv. 16, 19–20). Those dogs are one of the trivial yet real triggers that makes me ask myself, Do I really know who I am? Does my identity in Jesus Christ restrain my panic and anger? Am I able to hold on to myself? Or am I just "losing it"?

In the end, what I have learned is that my life is never entirely in my own hands. Despite my best efforts to practice the faith, I am still a weak human who calls out to God for help. I don't have my life all together. None of us ever will. We depend on a sustaining power from beyond ourselves that we can never simply command, plug in, or have at our disposal, but that nevertheless assures us, even when we have lost it, that God has not.

Confessing Hunger and Thirst

The Eucharist does not save us from all evil or harm. We will still have our moments of anger and panic, doubt and confusion. The Eucharist nevertheless bears a promise: that God will remember who we are, even when we have forgotten, and that God will find us, even when we are lost. This bread and wine make a meal to satisfy a hungry, thirsty people.

But the Eucharist can do us good only if we know that we are a hungry and thirsty people. We will learn thankfulness to God only if we know that we are dependent on God. If, on the contrary, we feel full spiritually, this bread and cup will only give us indigestion. If we think that we already have our lives all together, this bread and cup will only nauseate us. We will then be like the people of Israel in the wilderness. The quail that should have satisfied their hunger became repulsive to them. As Moses warned the people of Israel, "The LORD will give you meat, and you shall eat. You shall eat not only one day, or two days, or five days, or ten days, or twenty days, but for a whole month—until it comes out of your nostrils and becomes loathsome to you—because you have rejected the LORD" (Num. 11:18–20).

How do we come to learn that we are a hungry and thirsty people? Paradoxically, *not* by ignoring or neglecting the Eucharist. On the contrary, only as we participate in the Eucharist do we learn what it truly means to hunger and thirst for God. In the Eucharist, we learn that material and spiritual realities are deeply interconnected. God uses physical elements to lead us to heavenly truths. Those heavenly truths teach us to receive this earth and its material elements as God's precious gift to us. God has sanctified this world; he created it good, he came into it as human flesh, he rose in that body and appeared to his disciples, and he continues to use the things of this world to make himself known to us: water, bread, wine, and even the weak, seemingly powerless words of Scripture, sermon, and sacramental promise.

The Eucharist teaches us that we are spiritually hungry and thirsty, and so to give thanks again for God's "daily bread" to us. Yet, I fear, many of us are so satiated with the things of this world that we will not easily hunger and thirst for the things of God. If we have always had plenty to eat and drink at the kitchen table, will we be able to sit at the Lord's Table and receive the bread and wine as Christ's precious gift of himself? We are used to eating and drinking whenever we like, and as much as we want—so much so that half the American population is now obese.

Consumer society promises us every good thing here and now. Take the medieval cathedral by contrast. To enter the cathedral was to enter symbolically into a world beyond this world. The cathedral invited the worshiper to be lifted up to heaven and to contemplate eternal life. The divine light might already be radiating into this world, but it did not have its source in this world. The cathedrals of our times are the glistening shopping malls and "magic kingdoms" that promise us material abundance: clothes and entertainment, food and drink, company and service, fun and laughter, a world without crying or mourning all here and now. Why look heavenward, when we can make it all happen on earth? Why look to God, when all it takes are our concerted efforts and a strong economy?

In this context, even the call for more frequent Eucharist in mainline denominations raises troubling questions. It is true that these churches for too long emphasized the sermon and ignored the Eucharist. But are we now just acting like good American consumers who want to be able to stuff ourselves with Eucharist, just like McDonald's? Is our interest in Eucharist just one more expression of our conviction that we should be able to have all life's good things here and now, without waiting, without ever growing hungry and thirsty? Is the Eucharist teaching us thankfulness, or are we just learning to eat and drink whenever we like?

Fasting

Perhaps we have to learn again what it means to hunger and thirst physically, so that we can hunger and thirst spiritually. The monastic life is instructive. In most medieval monasteries that lived by the Rule of St. Benedict, people received sufficient food. In fact, the monasteries were such a reliable source of food that more than one person became a monk in order to guarantee himself his daily bread. But most of the year, the monks ate one time a day; only in the summer, when they worked long hours in the fields, might the abbot allow two meals. Whether one meal or two, there was never a breakfast, and thus never an experience of being filled and satisfied at the beginning of the day. Rather, the meals came later in the day—after people were hungry and thirsty. Each day, the monk lived a cycle of wanting and receiving, longing and being satisfied. Each day, the monk was reminded of his utter dependence on God.

Benedictine monasteries today have made various accommodations to the modern world, including three meals a day. But I recently spoke to a Benedictine nun who told me that one of the hardest adjustments for new members of her community is the rule against snacking between meals. Americans are so used to eating or drinking whenever we like that we no longer know much hunger or thirst and therefore do not know the joy and thankfulness that comes with having hunger stilled and thirst quenched. We are constantly filling ourselves, yet do not experience much satisfaction. We need to experience hunger and thirst.

Thus, it is significant that the Christian tradition has often required people to fast before receiving the Eucharist. The first food that they were to taste on the Lord's Day was the eucharistic bread and wine. They came to the table with physical hunger and thirst to remind them of their dependence on physical and spiritual nourishment from beyond themselves.

The need for training in hunger and thirst perhaps makes sense only for people who otherwise have enough—even too much—to eat and drink. I am not interested in romanticizing hunger and thirst. Hungry people need to eat. They do not first need to learn dependence; rather, they need to know that God will provide for them through those who have more than enough. But those who already have all too much to eat and drink must truly struggle with the words of Mary's Magnificat, that God "has filled the hungry with good things, and sent the rich away empty" (Luke 1:53). We are the ones who must learn hunger and thirst, so that what might first appear to be God's judgment (hunger and thirst) might show itself to be God's grace.

Self-Examination

While the sacramental relation between the material and the spiritual has led me first of all to explore disciplines of physical fasting, I believe that the Christian tradition has ultimately pointed to an even more profound spiritual discipline as preparation for participation in the

Eucharist: the practice of confession. When we confess our sins, we expose our spiritual hunger and thirst. When we admit to our failures and shortcomings, we acknowledge that we don't have our lives all together. When we honestly examine our lives with all their spiritual warts and blemishes, we finally say to God—and perhaps to each other as well—that we are utterly dependent on God to make our lives right and to give us our daily bread, the spiritual calories that sustain us in our baptismal identity.

The practice of confession asks us to be brutally honest, and such honesty is painful—so painful that, as Bonhoeffer and the community in Finkenwalde discovered, we would rather keep confession to ourselves. Self-examination, like the other practices and disciplines that we have investigated, takes a lifetime of time and effort—and the encouragement and accountability that only others in the community of faith can give us. We have to see where we have gone astray, where we have "lost it," and where we have therefore forgotten who we really are because we have denied our baptismal identity.

But confession is not only a matter of owning up to our failures to live out the Christian life. Confession is also a matter of declaring to God and others that we are fundamentally dependent people. Whatever power we have, we are ultimately powerless before forces of sickness and death. Whatever strength we have, we are finally weak in the face of trial and temptation. However Christian we like to think that we are, however much we practice the disciplines of the Christian life, we, like so many Christians over the centuries, finally have to confess:

> I do not understand my own actions. For I do not do what I want, but I do the very thing I hate. . . . For I delight in the law of God in my inmost self, but I see in my members another law at war with the law of my mind, making me captive to the law of sin that dwells in my members. Wretched man that I am! Who will rescue me from this body of death? (Rom. 7:15, 22–24)

The most difficult yet ultimately the most necessary confession is that I cannot live by my own efforts. I need God; I need others. I need life from beyond myself—plants and animals, mountain peaks and river valleys, a father and a mother, brothers and sisters in Christian faith, and even persons outside the Christian community to whom I am nevertheless connected by God's mysterious bonds.

Recovering Practices of Confession of Sin

As Dietrich Bonhoeffer discovered, confession must again become central to Christian existence. Ironically, we live in a world in which confession, in however distorted and self-serving a manner, is more apt to take place on television talk shows and in tabloid newspapers than in the church! Even the new mainline Protestant liturgies that restore the central place of the Eucharist to Lord's Day worship downplay confession. They emphasize, instead, the heavenly banquet and therefore the joy that the Eucharist offers us even now, and steer us away from a somber penitential tone that too often in the past held the Eucharist captive. But how without confession will we remember that we are hungry and thirsty people?

Unless we find meaningful and truthful ways to confess our sins, the food and drink that we receive at the Lord's Table will only condemn us to God's judgment (see 1 Cor. 11:29). North American Christians therefore face the profound challenge of learning to discipline themselves again as much in self-examination as in eucharistic celebration; both confession of sin and proclamation of forgiveness lie at the heart of our baptismal identity. The Eucharist holds them together and asks us to attend to both sides of the sacramental equation.

We can of course continue to ignore our need to confess sin. We can continue to pretend that we have no hunger, no thirst. But then we refuse to admit our dependency on God and others, and deny the fundamental fact that we cannot give ourselves life but, rather, have to receive whatever good we have from a source of life beyond ourselves. To live life before God without confession of sin is like trying to live off of our own physical bodies. We have undoubtedly stored up a few calories, and we can get along just fine for a while, but if we refuse to pay attention to our hunger, we will ultimately starve ourselves to death. So too, if we refuse to recognize our spiritual hungers and thirsts, we will finally fall spiritually exhausted, never knowing what hit us.

The Western church desperately needs to recover practices and disciplines of Christian confession, but I do not always know where we will find the brothers and sisters who will hear us and offer us God's self-giving love in word and deed. I too must still learn a great deal about confession. Only slowly have I come to learn over the years how difficult it is for me to maintain relationship with another person when something in the relationship burdens me and cries out for confession—whether relating to how much I have failed another or how much I still depend on him or her for love and life. More than once, I have gone to bed at night upset and agitated, needing to say something to my wife but not having the words or will. And more than once I have lain awake at night, until at two or three o'clock I knew that I had to make confession.

My wife is kind. She wakes up slowly and not without difficulty, but then she listens. (Ironically, when she is weighed down by her own need for confession, she sleeps excessively—and still wakes up the next morning as tired and restless as I after a night of lying awake!) When I think of the one thing that I most wish for my daughters, my precious ones, whom in baptism I have placed in the hands of the triune God, it is simply this: that they someday each have a spouse or friend who can be their confessor—and who will honor them by allowing them to hear his or her confession as well.

We will not participate in the Eucharist, the church's meal of thanksgiving, every day. But we can and must practice eucharist daily—"giving thanks" (which is the meaning of the original Greek, *eucharistein*). We must take time and make space each and every day to give thanks for the gift of life, the gift of new life in Jesus Christ, the gift of each other's presence, and the gift of these few years on earth. And we must learn to pause again and again, and to honor the God who is gracious and good and whose steadfast love endures forever.

Renewed practices and disciplines of confession will lead us into deeper thanksgiving. And perhaps renewed commitment to the Eucharist and daily thanksgiving for "health and strength and daily bread" will also make us hungry and thirsty for the ultimate things of God, even in the midst of our weakness and powerlessness—hungry and thirsty for life as children of the God who is Father, Son, and Holy Spirit. Hungry and thirsty to grow in our baptismal identity until that day when we feast with all God's people in heaven itself.

"Blessed are those who hunger and thirst for righteousness, for they shall be satisfied" (Matt. 5:6, RSV).

Notes

Introduction

1. For a provocative look at whether North American mainline churches have the spiritual resources to fulfill the vows that they make at baptisms, see Ronald P. Byars, "Am I Missing Something Here?" *Reformed Liturgy and Music* 29 (1995): 55–56.
2. The scholarly literature on this topic is now immense. For an overview of some of the issues, see Benton Johnson, Dean R. Hoge, and Donald A. Luidens, "Mainline Churches: The Real Reason for Decline," *First Things* 31 (March 1993): 13–18; and Wade Clark Roof and William McKinney, *American Mainline Religion: Its Changing Shape and Future* (New Brunswick, NJ: Rutgers University Press, 1987). More recent works by these sociologists are also helpful. A North American who has wrestled profoundly with the issue of Christian life and faith in a North American society in which Christianity is no longer "culturally established" is Canadian theologian Douglas John Hall. See, for example, *The Future of the Church* (Toronto: United Church Publishing House, 1989).
3. I borrow the term from the book by sociologist Wade Clark Roof, *Spiritual Marketplace: Baby Boomers and the Remaking of American Religion* (Princeton, NJ: Princeton University Press, 1999).
4. For example, Calvin treats the Christian life under the heading, "The Way in Which We Receive the Grace of Christ: What Benefits Come to Us from It, and What Effects Follow." See Calvin, *Institutes of the Christian Religion*, ed. John T. McNeill (Philadelphia: Westminster, 1960), 1:xiv.
5. On this point, the writings in recent years of theologian Stanley Hauerwas have been especially significant. See, for example, *The Peaceable Kingdom* (Notre Dame, IN: University of Notre Dame Press, 1983).
6. This sacramental way of framing the Christian life has been richly explored in recent years by Gordon Lathrop. See his *Holy Things: A Liturgical Theology* (Minneapolis: Fortress, 1993); and *Holy People: A Liturgical Ecclesiology* (Minneapolis: Fortress, 1999).
7. Two books of essays introduce key issues and the considerable literature: Dorothy C. Bass, ed., *Practicing Our Faith* (San Francisco: Jossey-Bass, 1997); and Miroslav

Volf and Dorothy C. Bass, eds., *Practicing Theology: Beliefs and Practices in Christian Life* (Grand Rapids: Eerdmans, 2002).

8. My reflections on the Ten Commandments are guided in particular by Reformed discussions, such as those in Calvin's *Institutes* and *Sermons on the Ten Commandments*, and in Reformed confessional documents, such as the Heidelberg Catechism and the Westminster Standards. I have also found rich guidance in the broader Christian tradition, especially in Luther's catechisms and in the Roman Catechism of 1566 (also known as the Catechism of the Council of Trent). Among more recent resources, I am especially indebted to Karl Barth's discussions in *Church Dogmatics*, III/4, and to the *Catechism of the Catholic Church* (1994).
9. Luther took this position. See "The Large Catechism," in *The Book of Concord*, ed. Theodore G. Tapert (Philadelphia: Fortress, 1959), 409–10.
10. See *The Catechism of the Council of Trent*, trans. John A. McHugh and Charles J. Callan (Rockford, IL: TAN Books and Publishers, 1982), 466. The notion of sin as wrong desire (concupiscence) is a legacy of Augustine's theology. See, for example, *The Confessions*, trans. Rex Warner (New York: New American Library, 1963), 183.

Chapter 1

1. *Book of Common Worship* (Louisville, KY: Westminster/John Knox, 1993), 411.
2. Martin Luther, "The Small Catechism," in *The Book of Concord*, ed. Theodore G. Tapert (Philadelphia: Fortress, 1959), 352.
3. Martin Luther, "The Large Catechism," in *The Book of Concord*, ed. Theodore G. Tapert (Philadelphia: Fortress, 1959), 446.
4. Dietrich Bonhoeffer, *Letters and Papers from Prison*, enlarged ed. (New York: Collier Books, 1971), 348.
5. For this review of Bonhoeffer's life, I draw extensively from Eberhard Bethge, *Dietrich Bonhoeffer: A Biography*, rev. ed. (Minneapolis: Fortress, 2000). See also the extensive editorial notes in Dietrich Bonhoeffer, *Life Together; Prayerbook of the Bible*, ed. Geffrey B. Kelley (Minneapolis: Fortress, 1996).
6. The university education included language instruction in Hebrew, Greek, and Latin, and course work in the classic theological disciplines.
7. Bethge, *Dietrich Bonhoeffer*, 427.
8. Bonhoeffer, *Life Together*, 27.
9. Ibid., 28.
10. Ibid.
11. As quoted in Bethge, *Dietrich Bonhoeffer*, 205.
12. Bonhoeffer, *Life Together*, 82.
13. Ibid., 62.
14. Ibid., 88.
15. Much of this work became the basis for Bonhoeffer's book *Discipleship*.
16. Bonhoeffer was an outstanding pianist and would sometimes play and sing.
17. In the words of one Reformation confession, by "ecclesiastical discipline . . . vice is repressed and virtue nourished." See "The Scots Confession," in *Book of Confessions* (Louisville, KY: Office of the General Assembly, Presbyterian Church [U.S.A.], 1994), 3.18 (chapter 18). Bonhoeffer treats the theme of church discipline more directly in *Discipleship*, ed. Geffrey B. Kelley and John D. Godsey (Minneapolis: Fortress, 2001), 270–75.

18. Bonhoeffer, *Life Together*, 95.
19. Ibid., 100–101.
20. Ibid., 104.
21. Ibid., 118. Bonhoeffer devotes the concluding and crowning chapter of *Life Together* to the Lord's Supper.
22. Compare *The Rule of St. Benedict*, trans. Anthony C. Meisel and M. L. Del Mastro (Garden City, NY: Image Books, 1975), 56–61.
23. Bonhoeffer, *Life Together*, 112.
24. Bethge, *Dietrich Bonhoeffer*, 465.
25. Bonhoeffer, *Life Together*, 112.
26. David Stubbs at Western Theological Seminary has explored the connection between practices and the work of the Holy Spirit in recent unpublished lectures.
27. See Dorothy C. Bass, ed., *Practicing Our Faith* (San Francisco: Jossey-Bass, 1997).
28. John Calvin, *Institutes of the Christian Religion*, 4.1.9; ed. John T. McNeill (Philadelphia: Westminster, 1960), 2:1023.
29. Ibid., 4.12.2, 2:1230.
30. See Charles Wiley, "Ordinary and Extraordinary Discipline," Church Issues Series, No. 6 (Louisville, KY: Office of Theology and Worship, Presbyterian Church [U.S.A.], 2003).
31. For eloquent reflections on how the church today might recover its identity in Word and sacrament, see Joseph D. Small, "A Church of the Word and Sacrament," in *Christian Worship in Reformed Churches Past and Present*, ed. Lukas Vischer (Grand Rapids: Eerdmans, 2003), 311–23.

Chapter 2

1. As the nineteenth-century Anglican theologian F. D. Maurice wrote, "If [the commandments] are *kept*, if they are watched over and thought about and cherished . . . they will give us an acquaintance with Him which we can obtain in no other way." See F. D. Maurice, *Reconstructing Christian Ethics: Selected Writings*, ed. Ellen K. Wondra (Louisville, KY: Westminster John Knox, 1995), 74.
2. Justin Martyr, "First Apology," in Early Christian Fathers, ed. Cyril C. Richardson (New York: Macmillan, 1970), 272 (chapter XLVI).
3. *The French Confession of 1559*, trans. Ellen Babinsky and Joseph D. Small (Louisville, KY: Office of Theology and Worship, Presbyterian Church [U.S.A.]), 17 (chapter XXXIX).
4. See, for example, Richard John Neuhaus, *The Naked Public Square: Religion and Democracy in America* (Grand Rapids: Eerdmans, 1984).
5. In the summer of 2003, Christian activists protested the removal of a Ten Commandments monument from the rotunda of the Alabama Supreme Court building.
6. See Stephen L. Carter, *The Culture of Disbelief* (New York: Doubleday, 1993).
7. Calvin is representative of the wider Christian tradition. See John Calvin, *Institutes of the Christian Religion* 2.8.1–12, ed. John T. McNeill (Philadelphia: Westminster, 1960), 1:367–79. The Westminster Larger Catechism also gives a nice summary of rules for right interpretation of the Ten Commandments. See "The Larger Catechism," in *Book of Confessions* (Louisville, KY: Office of the General Assembly, Presbyterian Church [U.S.A.], 1994), 7.209 (q. 99).

8. John Calvin, *Sermons on the Ten Commandments*, ed. Benjamin W. Farley (Grand Rapids: Baker, 1980), 153–54.
9. In Bard Thompson, *Liturgies of the Western Church* (Philadelphia: Fortress, 1961), 270–71.
10. Dietrich Bonhoeffer, *Life Together; Prayerbook of the Bible*, ed. Geffrey B. Kelley (Minneapolis: Fortress, 1996), 113.
11. "The Confession of 1967," in *Book of Confessions* (Louisville, KY: Office of the General Assembly, Presbyterian Church [U.S.A.], 1994), 9.13.
12. Luther likes to emphasize this point, as in "The Freedom of a Christian." See John Dillenberger, ed., *Martin Luther: Selections from His Writings* (Garden City, NY: Anchor Books, 1961), 68–69.
13. Dietrich Bonhoeffer, *Discipleship*, ed. Geffrey B. Kelley and John D. Godsey (Minneapolis: Fortress, 2001), 111–12.
14. Calvin, *Institutes* 2.7.12, 1:360. The origin of the term "third use of the law" is generally attributed to Philipp Melanchthon. See *Melanchthon on Christian Doctrine: Loci Communes 1555*, trans. Clyde L. Manshreck (New York: Oxford University Press, 1965), 127. See also the discussion in I. John Hesselink, *Calvin's Concept of the Law* (Allison Park, PA: Pickwick Publications, 1992), 38.
15. Calvin, *Institutes* 2.7.12, 1:361.
16. For the notion of command as permission, see Karl Barth, *Church Dogmatics*, II/2, ed. G. W. Bromiley and T. F. Torrance (Edinburgh: T. & T. Clark, 1957), 593. For Barth's interpretation of several of the Ten Commandments, see *Church Dogmatics*, III/4, ed. G. W. Bromiley and T. F. Torrance (Edinburgh: T. & T. Clark, 1961).
17. See Jan Milic Lochman, *Signposts to Freedom: The Ten Commandments and Christian Ethics*, trans. David Lewis (Minneapolis: Augsburg, 1982).
18. See Paul L. Lehmann, *The Decalogue and a Human Future: The Meaning of the Commandments for Making and Keeping a Human Future* (Grand Rapids: Eerdmans, 1995).
19. See Stanley Hauerwas and William H. Willimon, *The Truth about God: The Ten Commandments in Christian Life* (Nashville: Abingdon, 1999).
20. See Thompson, *Liturgies of the Western Church*, 198.
21. See Ilja M. Veldman, "Protestantism and the Arts: Sixteenth- and Seventeenth-Century Netherlands," in *Seeing beyond the Word: Visual Arts and the Calvinist Tradition*, ed. Paul Corby Finney (Grand Rapids: Eerdmans, 1999), 397–421. Note also that some Swiss Reformed churches combined font and table; at the time of the Lord's Supper, a board would be laid across the top of the font, thus expressing the intrinsic unity of the two sacraments.

Chapter 3

1. A key book is Dorothy C. Bass, *Receiving the Day: Christian Practices for Opening the Gift of Time* (San Francisco: Jossey-Bass, 2000).
2. See the entry for *šābat*, in *A Hebrew and English Lexicon of the Old Testament*, ed. Francis Brown, S. R. Driver, and Charles A. Briggs (Oxford: Clarendon, 1962), 991.
3. James L. Kugel, *The Bible as It Was* (Cambridge, MA: Belknap, 1997), 387.
4. Robert Goldenberg, "Law and Spirit in Talmudic Religion," in *Jewish Spirituality from the Bible through the Middle Ages*, ed. Arthur Green (New York: Crossroad, 1996), 243.

5. "A Brief Statement of Faith," in *Book of Confessions* (Louisville, KY: Office of the General Assembly, Presbyterian Church [U.S.A.], 1994), 10.1.
6. Jonathan Edwards, "A Divine and Supernatural Light," in *A Jonathan Edwards Reader*, ed. John E. Smith, Harry S. Stout, and Kenneth P. Minkema (New Haven, CT: Yale University Press, 1995), 119–20.
7. See Craig Barnes, "Savior at Large," *Christian Century*, March 13–20, 2002, 16.
8. See Paul Lehmann's reflections on language for God in *The Decalogue and a Human Future: The Meaning of the Commandments for Making and Keeping a Human Future* (Grand Rapids: Eerdmans, 1995), 101–44.
9. See Rowan Williams, *Lost Icons: Reflections on Cultural Bereavement* (Edinburgh: T. & T. Clark, 2000), 53–94. Williams, now the archbishop of Canterbury, offers trenchant insights into the cultural need for such free zones.
10. Karl Barth begins his theological ethics with an explication of the Sabbath commandment. See his *Church Dogmatics*, III/4, ed. G. W. Bromiley and T. F. Torrance (Edinburgh: T. & T. Clark, 1961), 47–72.
11. This theme is especially pronounced in Calvin's and Barth's treatment of the Sabbath commandment.
12. John Calvin, *Sermons on the Ten Commandments*, ed. Benjamin W. Farley (Grand Rapids: Baker, 1980), 104.
13. See Barth, *Church Dogmatics*, III/4, 67–72.
14. See John T. McNeill and Helena M. Gamer, eds., *Medieval Handbooks of Penance* (New York: Columbia University Press, 1938), 194.
15. Ibid., 205.
16. See "The Heidelberg Catechism," in *Book of Confessions* (Louisville, KY: Office of the General Assembly, Presbyterian Church [U.S.A.], 1994), 4.103 (q. 103: "Christian service to those in need"); and "The Larger Catechism," in *Book of Confessions*, 7.227 (q. 117: "works of necessity and mercy").
17. See Dietrich Bonhoeffer, *Life Together; Prayerbook of the Bible*, ed. Geffrey B. Kelley (Minneapolis: Fortress, 1996), 73.

Chapter 4

1. A notable exception is the work of a team of religious scholars under the direction of Don S. Browning. See Don S. Browning, *From Culture Wars to Common Ground: Religion and the American Family Debate* (Louisville, KY: Westminster John Knox, 1997). See also Marcia J. Bunge, ed., *The Child in Christian Thought* (Grand Rapids: Eerdmans, 2001).
2. See James M. Gustafson, *A Sense of the Divine: The Natural Environment from a Theocentric Perspective* (Cleveland: Pilgrim, 1994), 66.
3. The Hebrew word for *honor* includes connotations of heavy, weighty, and burdensome. See the entry for *kavod*, in *A Hebrew and English Lexicon of the Old Testament*, ed. Francis Brown, S. R. Driver, and Charles A. Briggs (Oxford: Clarendon, 1962), 457.
4. Already in the fifth century, Augustine saw this point clearly: "Domestic peace contributes to the peace of the city." Augustine, *The City of God*, ed. David Knowles (New York: Penguin, 1972), 876 (XIX.16).
5. *Book of Common Worship* (Louisville, KY: Westminster/John Knox, 1993), 406.
6. See, for example, Luther's comments to parents in "The Large Catechism," in *The Book of Concord*, ed. Theodore G. Tapert (Philadelphia: Fortress, 1959), 358–61.

7. See "The Westminster Larger Catechism," in *Book of Confessions* (Louisville, KY: Office of the General Assembly, Presbyterian Church [U.S.A.], 1994), 7.227–7.228 (qq. 117–18).
8. See Karl Barth's discussion of parents and children in *Church Dogmatics* III/4, ed. G. W. Bromiley and T. F. Torrance (Edinburgh: T. & T. Clark, 1961), 283.
9. Ibid., 249.
10. "The Scots Confession," in *Book of Confessions* (Louisville, KY: Office of the General Assembly, Presbyterian Church [U.S.A.], 1994), 3.01 (chapter 1).
11. "The Theological Declaration of Barmen," in *Book of Confessions* (Louisville, KY: Office of the General Assembly, Presbyterian Church [U.S.A.], 1994), 8.14 (thesis 2).
12. Dietrich Bonhoeffer, *Life Together; Prayerbook of the Bible*, ed. Geffrey B. Kelley (Minneapolis: Fortress, 1996), 100–101. See also the apostle Paul's frequent calls to mutual submission, as in Gal. 6:2 and Eph. 5:21.
13. For the story of Paul Burgess's missionary life, see Anna Marie Dahlquist, *Burgess of Guatemala* (Langley, B.C.: Cedar Books, 1985).
14. John Calvin, *Institutes of the Christian Religion* 4.1.1, ed. John T. McNeill (Philadelphia: Westminster, 1960), 2:1012.
15. See Charles Wiley, "Ordinary and Extraordinary Discipline," Church Issues Series, No. 6 (Louisville, KY: Office of Theology and Worship, Presbyterian Church [U.S.A.], 2003).
16. See Calvin, *Institutes* 2.8.38.
17. Augustine's reflections in Book 19 of *The City of God* continue to be instructive.
18. On his deathbed, the great Russian novelist Fyodor Dostoyevsky asked that the story of the prodigal son be read to his children, hoping that they would always remember their identity in Christ. See Joseph Frank, *Dostoevsky: The Mantle of the Prophet, 1871–1881* (Princeton, NJ: Princeton University Press, 2002), 748.
19. For beautiful reflections on this theme, see M. Craig Barnes, *Searching for Home* (Grand Rapids: Brazos, 2003).
20. *Book of Common Worship*, 912, 940.

Chapter 5

1. The series appeared between Dec. 15 and Dec. 24, 2002. For the treatment of the sixth commandment, see Chris Hedges, "Turning to Faith: An Ex-Vietnam Soldier, Now a Bishop, Deals with Blood on His Hands," *New York Times*, Dec. 20, 2002.
2. Biblical scholars note that the commandment in its original context did not apply to the killing of plants or animals, or to killing in self-defense. It "prohibits only that kind of antisocial killing, done in vulgar self-interest, that poses a threat to the very existence of the community." See the entry for "Ten Commandments" in *Harper's Bible Dictionary*, ed. Paul J. Achtemeier (San Francisco: Harper & Row, 1985), 1034.
3. John Calvin, *Sermons on the Ten Commandments*, ed. Benjamin W. Farley (Grand Rapids: Baker, 1980), 156.
4. Ibid., 161.
5. Ibid., 156.
6. See J. Glenn Gray, *The Warriors: Reflections on Men in Battle* (New York: Harper & Row, 1970).
7. Karl Barth incisively explores this point in his discussion of war. See Karl Barth, *Church*

Dogmatics, III/4, ed. G. W. Bromiley and T. F. Torrance (Edinburgh: T. & T. Clark, 1961), 451.

8. Members of the Social Gospel movement in the early twentieth century emphasized these social dimensions of sin. See, for example, Walter Rauschenbusch, *A Theology for the Social Gospel* (New York: Macmillan, 1917).
9. For a moving description of how a culture of violence deadens the spirits of children in inner cities, see Alex Kotlowitz, *There Are No Children Here: The Story of Two Boys Growing Up in the Other America* (New York: Doubleday, 1991).
10. Pope John Paul II has argued that all these forms of social violence are interrelated, and he has called on the church to oppose this "culture of death." For one discussion, see John Paul II, *Crossing the Threshold of Hope* (New York: Alfred A. Knopf, 1994), 204–11.
11. In the same way, after the Berlin Wall fell, the majority of East Germans celebrated their "liberation" rather than dwelling on their complicity in the communist system. See John P. Burgess, *The East German Church and the End of Communism* (New York: Oxford University Press, 1997), 105–21.
12. This theme has been powerfully developed by the twentieth-century Jewish philosopher Emmanuel Lévinas. Pope John Paul II appeals to Lévinas in interpreting the sixth commandment. See *Crossing the Threshold*, 210.
13. Calvin argues that each commandment of the second table vividly labels a broad category of sinful behavior. God gets our attention, so to speak, by presenting us with the worst-case scenario: murder. But having gotten our attention, God wants us to consider all behaviors that harm our neighbor. See John Calvin, *Institutes of the Christian Religion* 2.8.10, ed. John T. McNeill (Philadelphia: Westminster, 1960), 1:376.
14. My interpretation is indebted to the recently completed study catechism of the Presbyterian Church (U.S.A.). See *The Study Catechism* (Louisville, KY: Witherspoon, 1998), 67–68 (q. 115). See also George Hunsinger, "Social Witness in Generous Orthodoxy: The New Presbyterian 'Study Catechism,'" in *Reformed Theology: Identity and Ecumenicity*, ed. Wallace M. Alston Jr. and Michael Welker (Grand Rapids: Eerdmans, 2003), 327.
15. See Dietrich Bonhoeffer's essay, "What Is Meant by 'Telling the Truth'?" in Dietrich Bonhoeffer, *Ethics*, ed. Eberhard Bethge (New York: Macmillan, 1979), 363–72.
16. See Stanley Hauerwas and William H. Willimon, *Resident Aliens* (Nashville: Abingdon, 1989), 86–92.
17. Consult the statistics on the park's Web site: http://www.nps.gov/cuga/.
18. JSee John C. Mitchell, "Urban Sprawl: The American Dream?" *National Geographic*, July 2001, 48–73.
19. The fear that modern mass society was reducing people to mere material evoked the protest of some of the most important intellectual movements of the twentieth century. In different ways, Nietzsche, Kafka, Dostoyevsky, and Heidegger all asserted the radical freedom of the human in a dehumanizing world. See also Hannah Arendt's brilliant observations on mass society in *The Origins of Totalitarianism*, new ed. (New York: Harcourt Brace Jovanovich, 1973).
20. Fyodor Dostoyevsky, *The Brothers Karamazov*, trans. David Magarshack (New York: Penguin, 1958), 375.
21. Profound explorations of these issues appear in L. Gregory Jones, *Embodying Forgiveness: A Theological Analysis* (Grand Rapids: Eerdmans, 1995); and Miroslav Volf,

Exclusion and Embrace: A Theological Exploration of Identity, Otherness, and Reconciliation (Nashville: Abingdon, 1996).

22. Luther's theology of the cross reminds us that it is precisely in places of weakness and suffering that we meet the God who brings life out of death, something out of nothing. See Luther's Heidelberg Disputation, in *Luther's Works*, vol. 31, ed. Harold J. Grimm (Minneapolis: Augsburg, 1957), 39–58. Consult especially thesis 28.
23. The monastic life as described by St. Benedict is again instructive. Benedict recognizes that nothing is more important—and nothing is more difficult—for a Christian community than cultivating these patterns of mutual submission. See the prologue to *The Rule of St. Benedict*, trans. Anthony C. Meisel and M. L. Del Mastro (Garden City, NY: Image Books, 1975).
24. *Book of Common Worship* (Louisville, KY: Westminster/John Knox, 1993), 406.
25. Calvin, *Sermons on the Ten Commandments*, 165.
26. Calvin, *Institutes* 4.17.38, 2:1415.

Chapter 6

1. The third-century church father Origen gives what would become a classic spiritualized interpretation of this part of the Lord's Prayer. See *Prayer; Exhortation to Martyrdom*, trans. John J. O'Meara (Westminster, MD: Newman Press, 1954), 92.
2. See also John 7:37–38: "Let anyone who is thirsty come to me, and let the one who believes in me drink. As the scripture has said, 'Out of the believer's heart shall flow rivers of living water.'"
3. See Martin Luther, "The Small Catechism," in *The Book of Concord*, ed. Theodore G. Tapert (Philadelphia: Fortress, 1959), 353–54.
4. A rich and rewarding study of Calvin's sacramental theology is B. A. Gerrish, *Grace and Gratitude* (Minneapolis: Fortress, 1993). In the American Reformed tradition, a key work has been John Williamson Nevin, *The Mystical Presence* (Philadelphia: J. B. Lippincott, 1846). A reprint is available from Wipf and Stock Publishers, 2000.
5. "The Heidelberg Catechism," in *Book of Confessions* (Louisville, KY: Office of the General Assembly, Presbyterian Church [U.S.A.], 1994), 4.076 (q. 76).
6. John Calvin, *Institutes of the Christian Religion* 4.17.10, ed. John T. McNeill (Philadelphia: Westminster, 1960), 2:1370.
7. Ibid., 4.17.32, 2:1404.
8. For beautiful reflections on the significance of the Eucharist for everyday Christian life, see *The Journals of Father Alexander Schmemann, 1973–1983*, trans. Juliana Schmemann (Crestwood, NY: St. Vladimir's Press, 2000). Schmemann, an Orthodox priest and professor of theology, has helped North American mainline Protestants rediscover the centrality of the Eucharist.
9. See "The Scots Confession," in *Book of Confessions* (Louisville, KY: Office of the General Assembly, Presbyterian Church [U.S.A.], 1994), 3.21 (chapter 21): "Although the faithful, hindered by negligence and human weakness, do not profit as much as they ought in the actual moment of the Supper, yet afterwards it shall bring forth fruit, being living seed sown in good ground; for the Holy Spirit, who can never be separated from the right institution of the Lord Jesus, will not deprive the faithful of the fruit of the mystical action."
10. For a helpful analysis of this danger, see Amy Plantinga Pauw, "Attending to the Gaps

between Beliefs and Practices," in *Practicing Theology: Beliefs and Practices in Christian Life*, ed. Miroslav Volf and Dorothy C. Bass (Grand Rapids: Eerdmans, 2002), 33–48.

11. For interesting reflections on this point, see Rowan Williams, *Lost Icons: Reflections on Cultural Bereavement* (Edinburgh: T. & T. Clark, 2000), 139–87.

Index of Scripture

Index of Subjects and Authors